Words That
Heal

Words That
Heal

40 Encouraging Stories Inspired by James 3:1–12

Michael Ross & Brian Doyle

An Imprint of Barbour Publishing, Inc.

The authors are represented by and this book is published in association with the literary agency of WordServe Literary Group, Ltd., www.wordserveliterary.com.

Published by goTandem, an imprint of Barbour Publishing, Inc., P.O. Box 719, Uhrichsville, Ohio 44683, www.barbourbooks.com

Our mission is to publish and distribute inspirational products offering exceptional value and biblical encouragement to the masses.

Member of the
Evangelical Christian
Publishers Association

Printed in the United States of America.

Contents

Starting Point:
How to Live What James Taught

Imagine How Powerful Our Witness Could Be
If We Actually Learned to Tame Our Tongues!

Forty Years Ago: Another Day, Another Word Bullet

The jittery thirteen-year-old swung open the cafeteria doors, scanned the room, and then froze. A sharp, sickening pain jabbed at the pit of his stomach.

Day after day, the same thing, Keith thought. *I just can't handle this anymore.*

It wasn't the strange cafeteria smells that made him queasy. Keith knew he was about to face something far worse: the firing squad at the so-called cool kids' table.

"Oh, look who it is," blurted a sarcastic voice. "It's our best friend Keith. Come sit here, Keith—we've been waiting for you!"

The teen's heart began playing keyboards with his rib cage, and every muscle grew tense. He took a deep breath and stepped into the food line. Suddenly the same worn-out barrage of painful word bullets began to fly.

"Dork."

"Sissy."

"Wimp."

An empty milk carton smacked Keith on the side of his head, and laughter rose from the table. He squeezed his eyes shut.

Why does this stupid line have to go past these guys? Keith asked himself. *And why won't they leave me alone?*

Fast-Forward to the Present: Those Words Still Hurt

During meetings, Keith avoids eye contact with his boss. *Don't want her to call on me to answer questions,* he tells himself. *Just want to blend in and go stealth.*

Even as others at the table speak nonsense about issues within his expertise, Keith remains quiet. *I'll correct them later in an email.*

The fifty-three-year-old executive panics when public attention is focused on him, especially in a room filled with supervisors and vice presidents. His tongue gets tied and his heart races.

But remove the spotlight, and Keith suddenly shines.

It's crazy, he tells himself. *Why do I act this way? I get around crowds, especially during meetings, and I freeze up. It's as if I relive the cafeteria torture from when I was thirteen. Yet that was so long ago, and I'm not that zit-covered, scrawny kid anymore. But those words. To this day, I can still hear them—and they still hurt.*

A bit in the mouth of a horse controls the whole horse. A small rudder on a huge ship in the hands of a skilled captain sets a course in the face of the strongest winds. A word out of your mouth may seem of no account, but it can accomplish nearly anything—or destroy it!

It only takes a spark, remember, to set off a forest fire. A careless or wrongly placed word out of your mouth can do that. By our speech we can ruin the world, turn harmony to chaos, throw mud on a reputation, send the whole world up in smoke and go up in smoke with it, smoke right from the pit of hell.

This is scary: You can tame a tiger, but you can't tame a tongue— it's never been done. The tongue runs wild, a wanton killer. With our tongues we bless God our Father; with the same tongues we curse the very men and women he made in his image. Curses and blessings out of the same mouth!

My friends, this can't go on. A spring doesn't gush fresh water one day and brackish the next, does it? Apple trees don't bear strawberries, do they? Raspberry bushes don't bear apples, do they? You're not going to dip into a polluted mud hole and get a cup of clear, cool water, are you?

—James 3:3–12 MSG

The writer of this passage, James (a brother of Jesus), makes clear what most of us feel all too often: words can be cruel.

In fact, they can hurt—even destroy.

Unlike a gunshot or knife wound, reckless words can weaken a person's self-confidence. This includes those seemingly innocent cuts, slams, and jabs; those playful—but unkind and unflattering—labels we like to pin on others. We use them at church, in the workplace, in our families, and all throughout our communities. But the wounds caused by reckless words often don't heal for many years, if ever. They enter our ears and burrow themselves deep into our hearts. They may be stored deep in the mind, but they are never completely forgotten.[1]

Keith is a prime example. He isn't just a character we dreamed up. He's a *real* person who endured *real* pain. He claims the teasing he received as a child nearly messed up his identity. Check out the rest of his story:

"It got to a point where my own friends wouldn't even sit by me during lunch. We'd get to the cafeteria, and they'd conveniently disappear.

"So why did some of the guys at school give me such a hard time? I was a sensitive kid, and the girls liked me. Also, I was a Christian and didn't cuss or get into trouble. On top of that, I was a musician—not an athlete. In fact, I hated gym. I was the teen who was always picked last.

"By the end of my junior high years, I'd begun to think I was weird because I was creative and not athletic. What saved me was the support I got from my parents, my church, and my youth group.

"When I entered high school, I mustered up the courage to start a campus Bible study. I thought, *Okay, if the guys at school have already labeled me "weird," what will I lose by going all the way with my faith?*

"An amazing thing happened. When I accepted myself and did my best to be confident in the person God made me to be, I slowly gained acceptance from others—even from some of the guys who used to tease me."

Life definitely improved for Keith, but he admits that the wounds from the constant "word bullets" haven't fully healed. Sometimes they swirl through his brain and attack his confidence—usually when he steps into a meeting at work.

"God's still working on my life," he says. "He's impressed upon me the importance of using my speech positively; using words that will help heal the wounds of others."

Ready to Grow Your Spiritual Vocabulary?

This book can help you grow your spiritual vocabulary. Inspired by James 3:1–12 and filled with forty engaging stories and dozens of relevant scriptures, you'll learn how to use your speech positively—speaking kindness, sharing words that heal, expressing love, and praising God.

Four main topics guide the discussion: healing words for the *Church*, the *workplace*, the *family*, and the *community*. Read these pages on your own for personal reflection or use this book in a small group study. Better yet, gather the entire family and study *Words That Heal* together for the next forty days.

Each entry will spark conversation and spiritual growth using these sections:

- Healing Journey—inspiring stories
- Healing Steps—practical tips and scriptures to apply
- Healing Words for Growth—plenty of room to journal and personalize the content

And each section is filled with healing words for nearly every age, stage, and circumstance, as well as *Ready to Rethink* entries: four interactive studies that will help you apply God's healing words to your church, workplace, family, and community.

Let's get started.

Whoever of you loves life and desires to see many good days,
keep your tongue from evil and your lips from telling lies.
PSALM 34:12–13

The words of the reckless pierce like swords,
but the tongue of the wise brings healing.
PROVERBS 12:18

"If someone has a hundred sheep and one of them wanders off, doesn't he leave
the ninety-nine and go after the one? And if he finds it, doesn't he make far more
over it than over the ninety-nine who stay put? Your Father in heaven feels the
same way. He doesn't want to lose even one of these simple believers."
MATTHEW 18:12–14 MSG

Part One

Healing Words for the Church

1

Acting as If We've Been
Baptized in Lemon Juice
(and Other Ways We Repel People)

Follow God's example, therefore, as dearly loved children
and walk in the way of love, just as Christ loved us and gave
himself up for us as a fragrant offering and sacrifice to God.
EPHESIANS 5:1–2

Maybe you can't wait for Sunday to roll around. Maybe you attend a model church—a warm, welcoming place filled with smiling faces, kind words, healing ministry.

Chances are, you don't.

At goTandem and Back to the Bible, we're studying the spiritual lives of Christians worldwide—more than 150,000 men, women, and children to date. Know what we've learned about North American believers? More than 80 percent of us spend three months out of the year (a whole season) feeling burned out, beat up, and spiritually stuck.[1] And countless Christ-followers are just plain frustrated with church.

Unbelievable!

So if we asked you to list some of the things that bug you about your place of worship, what would you write? Here's what we've heard:

Top-Ten Reasons People Dread Sunday Mornings

10. Fake faith
9. Bad theology
8. Rejection
7. Hypocrisy
6. Worldliness

5. Cliques
4. Legalistic leaders
3. Uncaring pastors
2. Unkind Christians
1. Completely void of anything that remotely resembles Christ's love

In fact, some people are convinced that if Christ showed up at church in the flesh, He'd be ushered right out the front door. Do we care more about slick performances and marketing strategies than reaching the souls of the lost? Have our places of worship become cliquish, impersonal, depthless, mean-spirited, and lacking in genuine heart?

→ Take a moment to evaluate your church. What are its strengths and its weaknesses? What can you do to help make life better within your church family?

Healing Journey

Michael's Thoughts: "Christ + His People + Love = Church"

This simple formula accurately describes a church in Southern California that's near and dear to my heart. Step through the doors and its congregants greet you with smiles and hugs. And as you look around, you're instantly struck by the diversity of people: young and old, families and singles, rich and poor, professionals and blue-collar folks, extroverts and introverts, black, white, Asian, Latino, Native American.

It's like a little taste of heaven, I tell myself whenever I visit.

The worship is just as diverse and is always raw and real. No perfect voices or polished performances—just authentic praise to Jesus Christ. The preaching is alive and comes straight from the Word of God: "Consequently, faith comes from hearing the message, and the message is heard through the word about Christ" (Romans 10:17).

There's no ushering Jesus out the doors of this place. His Spirit is there every Sunday—in the worship, in the preaching, in the people!

"Christ's love changes everything," explains the pastor. "As people get their eyes off themselves and commit their lives to Jesus—especially to being imitators of Him—God's love begins to move through the entire sanctuary. There's no mistaking it!"

And that's exactly what the Lord wants: "Dear friends, let us love one another, for love comes from God. Everyone who loves has been born of God and knows God" (1 John 4:7).

Brian's Thoughts: "Give Me Sweet, Not Sour!"

Sometimes after a big Sunday lunch, I like to splurge and order dessert: a giant frosted sugar cookie, a slice of coconut cake, a scoop of French vanilla ice cream with chocolate sauce drizzled on top. Okay, I admit I have a sweet tooth—which means I have to exercise plenty of self-control throughout the week.

In addition to dessert, I enjoy a hot cup of coffee or a cold glass of tea, but I prefer to sweeten both. Recently I was in a coffee shop where a young woman ahead of me ordered her drink, "Extra light and extra sweet!" I was not acquainted with those terms, which seemed familiar to the person fixing the coffee, so I shifted slightly in order to see the ingredients. This large concoction received six generous doses of both cream and sugar. *Wow!* That's what I call a sweet drink!

So what do dessert and coffee have to do with that all-important activity that comes before Sunday lunch—church? I, like Michael, am convinced that the key trait of a healthy church is love. And I—just like most people—find myself repelled by Christians who act as if they've been baptized in lemon juice. Unfortunately, I've met plenty of them.

Who can forget the face of someone who just bit into lemon? The grimacing, the puckering, the sour expression. Now compare that to someone who just tasted the sweetest, smoothest slice of chocolate mousse cake!

Scripture tells us in Proverbs 16:24, "Gracious words are a honeycomb, sweet to the soul and healing to the bones." How do sweet words sound?

How do they bring sweetness to our soul?

We all know someone who always seems to have a pleasant word to share. This may be a family member or a close friend. You enjoy their presence and look forward to being around them. The words they speak may not be classified as "sweet," but the conversations with them always seem to bring a sweetness to your soul.

Although it is true that we may not need that cookie or ice cream after dinner or that honey in our tea, we need to hear pleasant words on a regular basis for the health and healing of our soul.

Healing Steps

Define how your church should look. For some clues, read Acts 6:1–8. Based on this passage, your church leaders—not to mention *everyone* in your congregation—should be filled with. . .

- God's Spirit
- God's wisdom
- God's faith
- God's grace
- God's power

Find ways to love people you may not like. First John 4:19–21 says, "We love because he first loved us. Whoever claims to love God yet hates a brother or a sister is a liar. For whoever does not love their brother and sister, whom they have seen, cannot love God, whom they have not seen. And he has given us this command: Anyone who loves God must also love their brother and sister."

Healing Words for Growth

Healing Words for My Family (and How I Plan to Use Them):

_____

_____

Healing Words for Growth:

_____

_____

_____

_____

Healing Words to Pray:

_____

_____

_____

_____

2

You Are the Church

You are no longer foreigners and strangers, but fellow citizens with God's people and also members of his household, built on the foundation of the apostles and prophets, with Christ Jesus himself as the chief cornerstone. In him the whole building is joined together and rises to become a holy temple in the Lord. And in him you too are being built together to become a dwelling in which God lives by his Spirit.
EPHESIANS 2:19–22

When you think of the word *church*, what images come to mind? Steeples, crosses, altars? Consider this: a church is not just a building. And what takes place inside is much more than a "well-timed Sunday service" or a "busy schedule of classes and socials."

As the apostle Paul explains in today's scripture passage, *you are the Church*, "built on the foundation of the apostles and prophets, with Christ Jesus himself as the chief cornerstone." And as a Christian, *you* are a holy temple—a dwelling in which God lives by His Spirit.

So, by itself, a church facility is just a bunch of bricks and windows and doors. But add to it the *real* holy temple—*you*—and the building becomes a *church*, a sanctuary inhabited by God Himself; a sacred house of worship where the Creator and the created commune.

→ **Describe the most meaningful church service you've ever experienced. What made it so memorable?**

Healing Journey

I (Michael) never quite grasped the truth that the Church is the people until I worshipped with some amazing Christians in Thailand. Believers in the hillside village of Musakee meet each week in a rustic open-air structure. Actually, their church building is nothing more than a thatched roof held up by several wooden poles. Beneath the lean-to are rows of makeshift pews, an altar, and a cross—no plush wall-to-wall carpet or air-conditioners or stained-glass windows.

Yet when Christians gather here to worship, God inhabits this place. Praises are sung, hands are lifted, scripture is read, prayers are spoken— and this simple shelter is transformed into one of the most beautiful sanctuaries I've ever seen.

→ **How would you describe your church—a crowded building or a holy family of believers? Is "the worship hour" for you more of a programmed experience each week—or is it a passion? And since you are the Church, why bother setting foot in a church building? After all, can't we worship God just as effectively on our own?**

Here's why fellowship with a body of believers is essential:

1. Attending church gives you a chance to worship with all kinds of people: young and old, rich and poor.

2. Church enables you to be fed from God's Word. Now you might say, "I get fed from the Bible all week; can't I have a day off?" And I would ask, what if your spouse (or parents) used that approach in cooking meals? "We feed you six days every week. Why don't you take a day off from eating? We don't want you to feel as if you're always in a kitchen environment." I don't think you'd be amused.

3. Going to church allows you to serve others. We should enjoy worship and study the Word (see Hebrews 10:24–25).

The choice is yours: keep Christianity as nothing more than a religion— keep it boring and dull by playing it safe, by going through the ceremonial motions and traditions of "churchianity"—or begin pursuing Jesus and His transforming *power*.

I don't know about you, but I want to take Jesus up on His promises. I want to step out and put His Word to the test in *all* areas of my life. So, for me, church is my training ground. I walk through the doors expecting to learn something new, to encourage others and to be encouraged. Most of all, I gather with other "holy temples," expecting to commune with my Creator.

Healing Steps

Don't settle for "churchianity." If you let Him, Jesus will take a dead, boring religion and transform it into something that is fresh and new, something that is exciting and full of life! That's what Christ came to do! He came to end "religion." That's right. He came to destroy meaningless ritual and replace it with a dynamic, on-fire *relationship*—a relationship with God Himself.

Don't allow church attendance to be a cure for insomnia. Jesus said, "I have come that they may have life, and have it to the full" (John 10:10). He did not say, "I've come to bore you out of your skull."

Do some soul searching today. Ask yourself a few questions: Is God the most important person in my life, or am I allowing other pursuits to push Him out of my life? Is church really boring, or am I just too tired to participate? Do I truly expect God to speak to me during a worship service, or am I just going through the motions?

Healing Words for Growth

Healing Words for My Family (and How I Plan to Use Them):

_____

_____

_____

Healing Words for Growth:

_____

_____

_____

Healing Words to Pray:

_____

_____

_____

3

Becoming a Master Builder

According to the grace of God given to me, like a skilled
master builder I laid a foundation, and someone else is
building upon it. Let each one take care how he builds upon it.
1 CORINTHIANS 3:10 ESV

Just look around your church. God has gifted the people you worship with in so many ways. Some are called to be pastors and teachers, others doctors and lawyers. Some are skilled mechanics, savvy businessmen, talented artists, brave soldiers—the list goes on and on.

I (Brian) hold so much respect for those who work in the engineering and construction trades. It fascinates me how a towering New York skyscraper can go from one person's idea to detailed plans to the finished structure—which, of course, involves thousands of tons of steel, concrete, and wires that are carefully pieced together through human ingenuity.

Amazing to think about, isn't it?

One day as I was studying the New Testament, another amazing thought captured my imagination: regardless of how God has gifted us, *we are all builders.* At least, that's what the apostle Paul tells us.

In the verse above, Paul is writing to the church in Corinth, telling them that he sees himself as a builder—a people builder. Throughout his ministry, he was intentional with relationships, doing his best to build up the Church, helping Christ-followers to grow in their faith.

But this isn't just a job for pastors. It's an assignment for every Christ-follower. Paul exhorted the Thessalonians to "encourage one another and build one another up, just as you are doing" (1 Thessalonians 5:11 ESV). Each person in Christ can build up the life of another through actions—and especially through words that heal.

→ Think about the words you use at church. Do they
build up others? Describe some specific ways that
you can build up the faith of your church family.

Healing Journey

When I was a young father, I spent countless hours lounging on the floor with my kids, playing with Legos. I call it *playing*, but for them it was building. Each child in my family had a different skill level and, of course, different ways of using his or her creativity.

I watched as one child meticulously snapped Legos into place as he carefully inspected his creation. "Here's the castle," he told his sister. "And these towers are where the soldiers guard the kingdom."

"I'm making a garden," chimed in the voice of another child. "This is where the food is grown for the king and queen."

Suddenly, before my eyes, a collection of white, red, and yellow bricks rose into an eclectic fortress—complete with medieval towers, battlements, and working catapults.

The imagination of a young mind is something to cherish! And today that same creativity is being expressed in many different ways within the Church. As a dad, it's exciting to applaud my kids as they grow and find their place in the body of believers.

"Just as a body, though one, has many parts, but all its many parts form one body, so it is with Christ" (1 Corinthians 12:12). Countless sermons, songs, and devotionals have been based on this scripture. But every Christ-follower has a God-given role. So where do you and your family serve? And how are you building up the body?

I'm usually distracted by trying to figure out which part of the body I am. I quickly think of the things I've done lately and try to place them into categories. Sometimes I chuckle as I think of some of the odd parts that I might be—the middle toe, an eyelash, or maybe even the belly button. But if I step back, away from my self-centered thoughts, I see a bigger picture. This passage isn't just about our actions and where we fit into the Church. It describes how we are created specifically and intentionally by our Creator.

We are not just a bunch of random humans who have been thrown into this world to bump around and fumble our way through life. We, each and every one of us, have been designed in the image of God. We all have a purpose and we fit together by His great design.

And as Paul reminds us, we are called to be "master builders," or rather "the Master's builders" within the body.

Healing Steps

What skill can you develop that will help build up another person? Here are some ideas:

Be observant. Take note and show interest in what is going on in a person's life. Ask questions.

Be affirming. Seek out what someone is doing well and note character qualities that are strong. Share them with the person in a way that affirms who they are.

Take the initiative. Start conversations and ask interesting questions. Communicate a genuine interest in another.

Be thankful. Appreciate and build up another by simply giving thanks to God and to that person for their friendship and the chance to know them.

Be eternal-minded. Building others up has an eternal impact.

Healing Words for Growth

Healing Words for My Family (and How I Plan to Use Them):

_____

_____

_____

_____

Healing Words for Growth:

_____

_____

_____

_____

Healing Words to Pray:

_____

_____

_____

_____

4

Hospital Mentality vs. Country Club Mentality

*There's nobody living right, not even one, nobody who knows
the score, nobody alert for God. They've all taken the wrong turn;
they've all wandered down blind alleys. No one's living right; I can't
find a single one. Their throats are gaping graves, their tongues slick
as mudslides. Every word they speak is tinged with poison. They open
their mouths and pollute the air. They race for the honor of sinner-of-
the-year, litter the land with heartbreak and ruin, don't know the first
thing about living with others. They never give God the time of day.*
ROMANS 3:10–18 MSG

As Christians, most of us say we believe in God's grace—at least in theory.

But as for living it out, well, that's a different matter. Too often we stigmatize those with life-controlling problems as we hide our own hang-ups; we bring down on each other an avalanche of unforgiving wrath—all in the name of *God's love*; we squelch our hope for change and render each other immobilized and neutralized by shame. Crazy, isn't it?

Maybe it's time to stop pretending and to start coming clean with each other. Everybody needs help—"There is no one righteous, not even one" (Romans 3:10). Maybe it's time to see the church as a hospital for us all, not a country club for the spiritually elite.

→ How would you describe your place of worship?
A hospital? A country club? Explain your answer. Think
about the "scary" people in the world: the homeless,
the addicted, the broken, the sick. How can you and your
congregation reach out to these people? What can you do
to make them feel welcome within your church family?

Healing Journey

Snapshot #1: "Don't Be Scared of Me"

Katherine has battled a lifetime addiction to alcohol and drugs. She has suffered many losses through the years. As a young woman, she lost her marriage and the respect of her two kids. She was even shunned by several churches she had turned to because, as Katherine puts it, "I smoke, and I don't fit their image of how a Christ-follower should look and act."

Yet this fifty-seven-year-old woman has given her heart to Jesus, and she desperately wants to know Him better.

She even wants to change.

"I just don't know how," she says. "I wish other Christians just weren't so scared of me. It's as if they think I'm going to track mud into the sanctuary. Well, at least you can clean the carpet. What about a human heart? Don't people matter more than buildings?"

Snapshot #2: "Don't Reject Me"

Forty-five-year-old Steve can relate. "If people knew about all the things that worry me, they'd think I'm crazy and that I lack what it takes to be a true Christ-follower," he says.

For Steve, anxiety moves from an occasional nuisance to a daily trial that binds his natural ability to cope in this world. "I worry about having a heart attack or think that something terrible might happen to my wife," he shares. "I worry about countless small things: *Did I lather up enough when I washed my hands? Do the cats like the food I bought?* And then I feel guilty about worrying—and fret about that, too. *Lord, what's happening to me?*"

But the thing Steve worries about the most is rejection. And that's exactly the thing he experiences most—at church.

• • •

Katherine and Steve aren't alone. Their stories bring up three key problems that every Christian must confront: We often go underground with our struggles because (1) we're afraid of being scorned by the Church, (2) we're convinced that we'll never measure up to what the Bible says about purity and holiness, and (3) we're clueless about how to handle our struggles in very practical, personal ways.

It's easy to feel loved by God when we have our act together. If we're able to do the "dos" and avoid the "don'ts" in life, our conscience is clear and we feel stronger, more acceptable, and certainly freer to approach Jesus. But what about those moments when we lose control? What about when we fail spiritually and embarrass ourselves—and those we love, when we disappoint our families, when we watch a dream shatter right before our eyes? What then?

And where's our church family? Right there by our side, encouraging us?

Despite the reality of sin, struggle, and pain in *every* believer's life, far too many Christ-followers drive sin underground. And that's pretty insane when you think about it!

We can be free from the bondage of sin, *and* we have the promise of eternal life with our heavenly Father who is absolutely crazy in love with us. And as a church, we can nurture the healing of our brothers and sisters. All we have to do is stop pretending that we have it all together. We must admit the stuff that has caused us to be stuck, take a gutsy step toward repentance, and trust that God will do His part.

We must leave the country club and check ourselves into the hospital—church.

Instead, we fake it, and, as pastor David Wilkerson points out, we bring others down with us:

> *We stigmatize people with life-controlling problems. We take away their character by thinking of them as hopelessly hooked. We are so offended by their practices, we have made their sins so scandalous, we turn them into outcasts with no hope of return. We help to destroy their hunger for God by bringing down on them an avalanche of reproach and unforgiving wrath.*
>
> *If you rob a sinner of his character, if you take away his dignity, if you focus only on his failures, if you treat him as a nonperson, if you*

shut off all his roads of retreat—he is driven to hardness. He becomes calloused and begins to fight back because that is all that is left for him. It is an easy step from hardness to violence. Humiliate the sinner, take away his sense of worth, and soon you will have driven him to total remorse. If there is no God in him to support him, he will lose all hope and finally give himself over to those who will accept him. Then he often uses that hostility as an excuse to remain in his sin.[1]

Healing Steps

Don't try to hide your sins. As believers, we must encourage and support each other and everyone who steps through the doors of the church. We nudge each other closer to Jesus, counting ourselves dead to sin and alive in Him. "Therefore do not let sin reign in your mortal body so that you obey its evil desires. Do not offer any part of yourself to sin as an instrument of wickedness, but rather offer yourselves to God as those who have been brought from death to life; and offer every part of yourself to him as an instrument of righteousness. For sin shall no longer be your master, because you are not under the law, but under grace" (Romans 6:12–14).

Let's view our places of worship as a hospital. Is it possible for each one of us to come clean with our own sin and actually learn to "carry each other's burdens" (Galatians 6:2)? What would this kind of community look like? It's exactly what a church is supposed to be—a safe place for people to tell their secrets and experience emotional and spiritual healing through faith in Jesus Christ.

Healing Words for Growth

Healing Words for My Family (and How I Plan to Use Them):

_____

_____

_____

_____

Healing Words for Growth:

_____

_____

_____

_____

Healing Words to Pray:

_____

_____

_____

_____

5

Creating a Safe Harbor for Everyone

*The Son is the radiance of God's glory and the exact representation
of his being, sustaining all things by his powerful word.*
HEBREWS 1:3

"Anyone who has seen me [Jesus] has seen the Father."
JOHN 14:9

What is God's character like? We can find the answer to that question by looking to Jesus, for he is the exact representation of God the Father.

Through the ages, the nature and character of God have been described in countless ways—holy, compassionate, merciful, gracious, loving, faithful, forgiving—just to name a few. One essential character trait that all of humanity can celebrate is *giving*. We have life only because God has created us by an exercise of His will. We can receive salvation only because He has willed to grant it.

God's heart never stops giving. It is because of His nature that we are able to approach Him. "Your voice matters in heaven," writes author Max Lucado. "[God] takes you very seriously. When you enter His presence, He turns to you to hear your voice. No need to fear that you will be ignored."[1]

Do you see God this way? When you think of Him, what images come to mind?

Is He an impersonal judge, banging His gavel—sentencing you to "life without parole"? Could He be "the unapproachable burning bush that Moses encountered"? Is He simply a spirit? A loving father? Maybe a bearded Jesus with dirty sandals and sun-burned skin? Who is He to you? Who is He to your church?

→ **How does your view of God change as you study His Word? How do your daily circumstances filter your perception of the**

Almighty? Why is it so important to have an accurate view of God? In what ways can the wrong view of God keep people from coming to church?

Healing Journey

Before I (Michael) committed my life to Christ, I had come to some very selfish and immature conclusions about the life of faith. To begin with, I judged all Christians by the few churches I had encountered—which, at the time, seemed to be filled with loud, weird, legalistic people who only knew two words: "don't" and "never."

And I didn't feel as if I could ever fit in or measure up. So I reasoned that since I couldn't live the pure life in my actions, I wouldn't try. *Church is a holy club for the spiritually elite—a place where people look down on sinners. I don't want any part of that.*

But after I committed my life to Christ and began to look deeper at faith (and the Church), I found that God wasn't a God of debits and credits; He was an unconditional lover of those who humbly admitted their own sin and who genuinely realized they needed the Savior.

If we could in humility think and say, "God be merciful to me, a sinner," then He would be more than happy to oblige for us.

Through the years, as I grow closer to Jesus, here's what I'm beginning to conclude each day: God's love is something we can't quite grasp—and will never fully understand. At least in this life. And because of God's love, He forgives our sin through Jesus Christ and graciously brings us back into fellowship with Him. Abandoning His unholy, imperfect children is unthinkable to God—just as it was unheard of to the father of the prodigal son.

The simplicity of God's love is wonderful and awesome. Both creation and salvation have their own depth of wonder, to be sure. But the daily love and concern God has for His children is truly *awe*-some.

As for church, it's still pretty weird! Good weird. And I seem to fit right in. While it isn't perfect, it is a safe harbor where all who come are loved and accepted and are given every opportunity to experience God's mysteriously amazing, giving heart.

•••

A safe harbor is what I (Brian) experience at my church, too. Let me give you a simple example of what I observe.

My friend Dan often comes alongside me and puts his hand on my shoulder, declaring, "You're the best." I don't know what I am the best at, but I like hearing Dan say it. Recently I saw him do the exact same thing to another friend of mine. He put his hand on his shoulder and repeated the same words. Then he did it later with another person. Wait a minute—how can we all be the best?

Every once in a while Dan will come alongside someone and say, "You're God's best." He is not attempting to give empty praise, but rather to provide something that is lacking for most of us.

When was the last time someone praised you for who you are? When have you done this for the folks you worship with—perhaps even perfect strangers who step through your doors?

I love to compliment my children, and I remember a family friend heard me offer unsolicited praise to my daughter for nothing she had done but for simply who she was. My friend remarked that I might want to be careful because my child might become conceited. She might become convinced that she is truly better than others and treat people accordingly.

Certainly the scriptures encourage each of us to intentionally grow in the area of humility and to seek to become a humble person. James and Peter both write in their letters that "God opposes the proud but shows favor to the humble" (James 4:6; 1 Peter 5:5). Jesus warns in Matthew 23:12, "Those who exalt themselves will be humbled, and those who humble themselves will be exalted."

While these are strong instructions regarding humility, it doesn't mean that God discourages the affirmation of others. Quite the opposite. Life itself can be very humbling, and the longer you live, the more humbling it can become. Nurture a safe harbor in your church (and family). Be generous with kind, healing words.

Healing Steps

We see God the Father offer unsolicited praise to God the Son in Matthew 3:17 before Jesus had even begun His ministry season. He offered it loud and clear so that others might hear as well, saying, "This is my Son, whom I love; with him I am well pleased." God did not wait until Jesus did something spectacular to praise him in public. God also did not seem concerned that some unsolicited praise might swell Jesus' head. He praised Him and gave us a model we can follow.

When I offer praise to my daughter or another family member or to friends at church, I have the difficulties of life in mind. Offering unsolicited praise can be a powerful resource in a few different ways:

1. Offering unsolicited praise can build someone up so that they do not feel like they need to declare their own praises. Proverbs 27:2 says, "Let someone else praise you and not your own mouth; an outsider, and not your own lips."

2. Offering unsolicited praise can help build a reservoir of confidence to try new things and not be afraid of failure. The most likely person to see the upside of a risky opportunity is the person who thinks they can do it and that it will work out.

3. Offering unsolicited praise can also help people become resilient when life deals them an unexpected blow and circumstances do not work out as hoped.

Healing Words for Growth

Healing Words for My Family (and How I Plan to Use Them):

_____

_____

_____

_____

Healing Words for Growth:

_____

_____

_____

_____

Healing Words to Pray:

_____

_____

_____

_____

6

Seeing Christ in Our Words and Deeds

*My life is worth nothing to me unless I use it for finishing
the work assigned me by the Lord Jesus—the work of telling
others the Good News about the wonderful grace of God.*
ACTS 20:24 NLT

Who do you think of when you read the words "reflecting His love" and "doing His work"? Images of Mother Teresa and Jim Elliot flash through my mind. The ubiquitous cliché "What would Jesus do?" feels like the right question to ask when confronted with a situation that calls for His love.

Yet you may say to yourself, *I could never willingly preach the gospel to a cannibalistic tribe. I hope God never asks me to live in poverty.*

Some will never know the supernatural boldness given by God to accomplish the difficult tasks He asks of us. Others already have experienced His overflowing measure of love and grace spilling over to everyone around. However, you may be one still wondering if given extreme circumstances, if you would you be able to reflect His love.

> → Do others see Jesus in your words and deeds?
> Explain your answer. When does it come easy?
> When is it hard?

Healing Journey

I (Brian) want to introduce you to someone who happens to be my best friend.

We knew each other for a long time, but we didn't start to get close until college. That was when I decided to talk to him more than offering a friendly greeting or an occasional thank-you when helped in one way or another. Gradually we began to talk briefly a few times a week. He had written me letters, which I would read at night and fall asleep to his caring words. Another friend of mine noticed something different about me. He said that I seemed at peace and had more confidence.

My friend is the best listener and gives the best advice. Through the years, I have taken my struggles to him—anything and everything: frustrations over a broken relationship or a job that didn't work out. Every time, I'd come away with peace, knowing that God is still taking care of me. He always reminds me how faithful God is to accomplish the plans He has for me. He says he prays for me, especially when I don't know how to pray. I can always trust him at his word.

It is because of him that my other friendships are so close. It is because of his encouragement to me that I can encourage other people. His generosity toward me makes me want to be generous to others. His compassion, kindness, love, and faithfulness to everyone spur me on to be the same. I want to be just like him.

My best friend, you may have guessed, is the Lord Jesus Christ. My faith in Him becomes more real the more I make Him a part of my life.

I want others to see Him in my words and deeds. This is the true work God has for each one of us. No need to be a Mother Teresa or a Jim Elliot. I just need to be me.

And when my friends see Jesus reflected in my life, it doesn't matter if we are separated by great distances. They'll still remember seeing Jesus in our lives. I'll still remember seeing Him in their lives, and the connection will remain strong.

• • •

I grew up in New England and lived there for more than fifty years before moving with my family to the Southeast. My wife and children especially missed the personal touch face-to-face visits with those we know well brings.

We, too, had experienced people moving away to various places, but this happened one relationship at a time—never dramatically impacting our own relational network. There were always multiple people who remained with whom we had significant history. In fact, there was a somewhat positive side to seeing people move on, as we could experience to a small extent their adventure with them.

My wife and I were very intentional in shepherding our five children through transitional time, and we worked hard to build family unity. Different people make friends at different speeds, and our family was no exception. Courage and steps of faith were needed to initiate friendships and to get acquainted with people we did not know.

Proverbs 25:25 shares, "Like cold water to a weary soul is good news from a distant land." The photos and handwritten cards and letters from people we knew well but had not seen were so refreshing to us.

The refreshment did not come just because there was some good news. That was part of it. We enjoyed hearing the positive things that had happened in the time we had been away. The refreshment did not come just because the news was from a distant land. After all, in the twenty-first century, we can be engaged with news about literally any area of the world in a moment's time. The refreshment did not come just because we were weary. The change we experienced was enormous and took a major investment of emotional, mental, and physical energy. I think the refreshment came because of all those reasons together. New friendships were being born and cultivated but could not provide the same touch that an old friend could supply.

Know what helped? The bond we share in Christ Jesus. We've seen Him in the lives of our old friends, and we're seeing Him in the lives of our new ones.

This is "the work of telling others the Good News about the wonderful grace of God."

Healing Steps

Let your life reflect God's love to others. Remember it is not your own reflection of love that people will see; it is God's love in you. Real faith demonstrates to the world real love. Love is an action, not an emotional high. To get a general sense of what God's love looks like in everyday life, meditate on 1 Corinthians 13 and 1 John.

Learn what real faith is by spending as much time with God as possible. Ask Him for wisdom in a new relationship; learn what His voice sounds like when He speaks to you. In Philippians 4:6, Paul urges his readers, "Do not be anxious about anything, but in every situation, by prayer and petition, with thanksgiving, present your requests to God." I take that very literally. I want to come to a point where I am not anxious about the outcomes of my decisions because I have assurance that I have discussed the situation with my Lord, and He has led me in the direction He wills. Therefore, I pray and tell the Lord every request and question I have. He'll answer me one way or another—possibly not the way I would like, but His way is always best.

Healing Words for Growth

Healing Words for My Family (and How I Plan to Use Them):

_____

_____

_____

_____

Healing Words for Growth:

_____

_____

_____

_____

Healing Words to Pray:

_____

_____

_____

_____

7

Navigating the Fear Factor

*"Do not fear, for I have redeemed you; I have summoned you by name;
you are mine. When you pass through the waters, I will be with you;
and when you pass through the rivers, they will not sweep over you.
When you walk through the fire, you will not be burned; the flames
will not set you ablaze. For I am the LORD your God,
the Holy One of Israel, your Savior."*
ISAIAH 43:1–3

Fear. Cold, clammy, bone-chilling fear. For some Christians, it's a way of life: *Lord, I'm trapped. I feel lost and alone and scared. Scared of being rejected, of losing control, of facing the future, of risking my heart, of surrendering my life to You.*

A healthy fear of the Lord—the kind that is rooted in respect and reverence for Him—is actually pleasing to God. But our Savior wants to drive out worldly fear—the sort that stems from doubt and condemnation, the type that leaves its victims panicked and paralyzed and ineffective for service in God's kingdom.

The Lord wants to build in you the courage needed to walk boldly with Him. Charles H. Spurgeon explains it this way:

> *You will need the courage of a lion to pursue a course that could turn your best friend into your fiercest foe. For the sake of Jesus Christ, you must be courageous. Risking your reputation and emotions for the truth requires a degree of moral principle that only the Spirit of God can work into you. Do not turn back, do not be a coward; be a hero of the faith. Follow in your Master's steps. He walked this rough way before you.*[1]

Are uncontrollable fears threatening to flatten your faith? Do you catch yourself shaking in your boots instead of standing strong for Christ?

Healing Journey

Imagine if a surge of raw courage flowed through your veins—even in the deadly grip of a lion's fangs. Daniel knew this degree of courage (see Daniel 6:22–27).

Despite the order not to pray, Daniel remained committed to God. After all, he'd seen the Master's hand move in amazing ways—especially the time when three fellow believers were thrown into a blazing furnace. The flames were so hot that King Nebuchadnezzar's soldiers died as they threw Shadrach, Meshach, and Abednego into the fire. Yet the men of God stepped out of the furnace unharmed. Not a single hair on their heads was singed!

"Praise be to the God of Shadrach, Meshach and Abednego," Nebuchadnezzar proclaimed. "They trusted in him and defied the king's command and were willing to give up their lives rather than serve or worship any god except their own God" (Daniel 3:28).

Now, many years later, the opposition to God and His people continued. This time Babylon's administrators had convinced the new king, Darius the Mede, to issue a crazy decree: "Anyone who prays to any god or human during the next thirty days, except to you, Your Majesty, shall be thrown into the lions' den" (Daniel 6:7).

Daniel didn't flinch. He knelt at his upstairs window—the one opened toward Jerusalem—and prayed three times a day, giving thanks to God, just as always.

"Did you not publish a decree?" the administrators asked the king.

"The decree stands," the ruler replied, and Daniel was quickly thrown into the lions' den (6:12).

"May your God, whom you serve continually, rescue you!" the king told Daniel (6:16). Then a stone was placed over the mouth of the den.

Was Daniel's life about to end with the fierce swipe of a lion's paw? Not a chance! Just as with the miracle in the furnace, God protected and prospered His obedient child.

Daniel emerged unscratched, and King Darius was overjoyed: "For [the God of Daniel] is the living God and he endures forever. . . . He rescues and he saves; he performs signs and wonders in the heavens and on the earth. He has rescued Daniel from the power of the lions" (6:26–27).

The same almighty, all-powerful, eternal God will rescue you from the struggles you face. He will drive out worldly, paralyzing fear and will replace it with raw courage—if you will trust Him.

Healing Steps

Allow Jesus to drive out fear. After all, Christ came to rescue us from the fear of sin, of death, even of hell. God sent His Son to save us from all of that. If we choose to believe in Jesus, we won't die; we'll receive eternal life. That truth alone should drive out fear!

Don't buy a lie. Jesus wants you to recognize sin and the lies of this world. He wants you to have the courage to stand up and say, "That's just not right." The next time you're full of fear and in a tight spot, ask yourself this question: "Am I willing to throw away what's right and settle for actions that are wrong—just to please people?"

Healing Words for Growth

Healing Words for My Family (and How I Plan to Use Them):

_____

_____

_____

_____

Healing Words for Growth:

_____

_____

_____

_____

Healing Words to Pray:

_____

_____

_____

_____

8

Loving Words for Unlovely People

*The pessimist complains about the wind; the optimist
expects it to change; the realist adjusts the sails.*
WILLIAM ARTHUR WARD[1]

"Let's Strive to Get Along"

Ephesians 4:25: "Therefore each of you must put off falsehood and
speak truthfully to your neighbor, for we are all members of one body."

A Kind Response: Express your desire to promote peace.

"Let's Strive to Love Others"

Ephesians 4:15–16: "Speaking the truth in love, we will grow to become
in every respect the mature body of him who is the head, that is, Christ.
From him the whole body, joined and held together by every supporting
ligament, grows and builds itself up in love, as each part does its work."

A Kind Response: Express your desire to share Christ's love.

"Let's Strive to Serve Together"

Romans 12:4–5: "Just as each of us has one body with many members,
and these members do not all have the same function, so in Christ we though
many, form one body, and each member belongs to all the others."

A Kind Response: Express your desire to tear down walls and to serve
in unity. Point out that each of us performs a different function within
the Church, but ultimately we are part of the same body of believers.

Christ-Followers, Plant These Words and Grow

Nourish spiritual growth with God's Word. Growing in faith and learning
to coexist with difficult people means having the ability to "forget what lies
behind" (see Philippians 3:13) and "throw off everything that hinders and

the sin that so easily entangles" (Hebrews 12:1). It means being willing to forgive our brother or sister and to humbly ask God each day to clean out the pipeline between Him and us so we can start fresh. The Bible tells us the truth about yesterday's sins: "I will forgive their wickedness and will remember their sins no more" (Jeremiah 31:34).

Listen to the words of a healing believer who has been hurt by unloving Christians countless times. "There are a lot of broken people in this world. I'd say that *all* are broken, but only a few admit it. We like to believe we're okay—that we have it all together; it makes us feel better about ourselves. I've learned that it's okay to be broken. When we get to this point, we can put away all the junk that gets in the way—our efforts to 'get things right,' and to 'do Christian things'. . .our pride, our stubborn wills, our attempts to control everything and everyone. God is our Healer. He can accomplish in us what we cannot do on our own."

In the days ahead, do the following:

Plot a course for growth. List your goals:
 In one month I want to. . .
 In six months I want to. . .
 In one year I want to. . .

List ten steps that you will take to grow (and reach your goals above):

1. _____
2. _____
3. _____
4. _____
5. _____
6. _____
7. _____
8. _____
9. _____
10. _____

9

Loving Words for Laymen and Leaders

*Why am I afraid to dance, I who love music and rhythm
and grace and song and laughter? Why am I afraid to live, I who love
life and the beauty of flesh and the living colors of the earth
and sky and sea? Why am I afraid to love, I who love love?[1]*
EUGENE O'NEILL

"I Honor Your God-Ordained Authority"

Hebrews 13:17: "Have confidence in your leaders and submit to their authority, because they keep watch over you as those who must give an account. Do this so that their work will be a joy, not a burden, for that would be of no benefit to you."

An Encouraging Word: Express how thankful you are for the wisdom and authority God has given your church leadership.

"I'll Support You on the Journey"

Romans 12:1–2 (MSG): "So here's what I want you to do, God helping you: Take your everyday, ordinary life—your sleeping, eating, going-to-work, and walking-around life—and place it before God as an offering. Embracing what God does for you is the best thing you can do for him. Don't become so well-adjusted to your culture that you fit into it without even thinking. Instead, fix your attention on God. You'll be changed from the inside out. Readily recognize what he wants from you, and quickly respond to it. Unlike the culture around you, always dragging you down to its level of immaturity, God brings the best out of you, develops well-formed maturity in you."

An Encouraging Word: Express how thankful you are for the sacrifices your church leaders have made for your congregation. Explain that you share in Christ's mission.

"Jesus Has Called Me to a Surrendered Life"

Matthew 16:24–26: "Whoever wants to be my disciple must deny themselves and take up their cross and follow me. For whoever wants to save their life will lose it, but whoever loses their life for me will find it. What good will it be for someone to gain the whole world, yet forfeit their soul? Or what can anyone give in exchange for their soul?"

An Encouraging Word: Express how thankful you are for the sacrifices your church leaders have made for your congregation. Explain that you share in Christ's mission.

Christ-Followers, Plant These Words and Grow

Nourish spiritual growth with God's Word. In Bible times, a centurion's boots were broken in and carefully cared for. They were as much a comfort during long days of travel as they were a protection in battle.

Today way too many Christ-followers, lay leaders and pastors included, become weary and discouraged during their Christian service when it becomes a hard, long, uphill trek—and especially when they feel very little support from church boards and congregants. But the message of Jesus is the good news of *peace,* not pain. He put it this way: "Come to me, all you who are weary and burdened, and I will give you rest. Take my yoke upon you and learn from me, for I am gentle and humble in heart, and you will find rest for your souls. For my yoke is easy and my burden is light" (Matthew 11:28–30).

Rest? Easy? Light?

If we're convinced the Christian life is wearisome, hard, and heavy, that's exactly what we'll experience. In those moments of navel-gazing discouragement, we don't have our combat boots on. We're walking thorny ground in bare feet. Connect with Jesus. He's everything we need: our truth, our righteousness, our peace, our rest. The journey with Christ is not short, and sometimes it's dangerous, but it's an adventure that's meant to be enjoyed.

In the days ahead, do the following:

Plot a course for growth. List your goals:
In one month I want to. . .
In six months I want to. . .
In one year I want to. . .

List ten steps that you will take to grow (and reach your goals above):
1. _____
2. _____
3. _____
4. _____
5. _____
6. _____
7. _____
8. _____
9. _____
10. _____

10

Ready to Rethink Church and Start Living What Christ Intended?

Now we ask you, brothers and sisters, to acknowledge those who work hard among you, who care for you in the Lord and who admonish you. Hold them in the highest regard in love because of their work. Live in peace with each other. And we urge you, brothers and sisters, warn those who are idle and disruptive, encourage the disheartened, help the weak, be patient with everyone. Make sure that nobody pays back wrong for wrong, but always strive to do what is good for each other and for everyone else.
1 THESSALONIANS 5:12–15

Let's Chart a Healing Path toward Change

1. *Receive God's Word.* Read or listen to Ephesians 2:11–22.

2. *Reflect on Ephesians 2:19–22.* Pull these verses apart sentence by sentence, looking for God's personal message to you. Invite the Holy Spirit to speak to you.

> *Consequently, you are no longer foreigners and strangers, but fellow citizens with God's people and also members of his household, built on the foundation of the apostles and prophets, with Christ Jesus himself as the chief cornerstone. In him the whole building is joined together and rises to become a holy temple in the Lord. And in him you too are being built together to become a dwelling in which God lives by his Spirit.*

3. *Engage in a conversation with God.* After a moment of silence before the Lord, write out a dialogue between you and Him. Begin with general thoughts and impressions.

Heavenly Father, here's how I feel about these verses:

_____

_____

_____

_____

Here's what's hard for me, God—what I don't understand:

_____

_____

_____

_____

Now relate these verses to your specific circumstances.

Here's what Ephesians 2:11–22 is telling me about Your Church and the important part I have in it:

_____

_____

_____

_____

With your help, Lord, here's how I'll try to rethink Church and reconnect with it:

_____

_____

_____

_____

4. *Memorize Ephesians 2:13–14.* Repeat it to yourself as often as needed. Write it on an index card and post it within sight.

But now in Christ Jesus you who once were far away have been brought near by the blood of Christ. For he himself is our peace, who has made the two groups one and has destroyed the barrier, the dividing wall of hostility.

5. *Respond to God's nudges.* Try this "church connection" exercise:
   - *Evaluate your church experience.* Back in college, before I (Michael) became a Christian, one of my biggest stumbling blocks was the hypocrisy I saw in certain so-called "followers of Christ." At times I couldn't help feeling that church was just a building full of angry, finger-pointing people. Where was the hope? Where was the unity in Christ? Then I met a guy named Scott. Not only did he claim to be a Christian, but he actually lived his faith. Scott was real. He was strong in his convictions, yet he didn't try to hide his weaknesses. And I never felt judged by him. In fact, the more time I spent with Scott, the more I began to sense the presence of Christ. My friend even led me in prayer the day I committed my life to Jesus. I'll always remember one of his first pieces of advice: "Get your eyes off other Christians because they'll sometimes let you down. Even I'll disappoint you. Instead, focus on Jesus. Trust Him, follow Him—and do all you can to be like Him." I took my friend's advice. Instead of getting angry or giving up, I decided to look for the "Scotts" in my church and to do my best to follow what they did—reflect Christ's face.

What frustrates you about church? _____

_____

_____

What can you change? _____

_____

_____

*Why is it so important to get connected within a Christian community, especially as you fight temptation and sin?*_____

_____

_____

*Who are the "Scotts" in your church?*_____

_____

_____

In what ways can you be a "Scott" to others? _____

_____

_____

- *Evaluate your service to others.* Here's what Mother Teresa once said about carrying each other's burdens: "We all long for heaven where God is, but we have it in our power to be in heaven with him right now—to be happy with him at this very moment. But being happy with him now means: loving as he loves, helping as he helps, giving as he gives, serving as he serves, rescuing as he rescues, being with him for all the twenty-four hours, touching him in his distressing disguise."[1]

How does caring for others help you with your own sin battle? _____

_____

_____

Part Two

Healing Words
for the Workplace

11

It's Time to Be a Cubicle Missionary

Whatever you do, whether in word or deed, do it all in the name of the Lord Jesus, giving thanks to God the Father through him.
Colossians 3:17

Work. How should Christians view their source of income? How should they define it? What should their attitude be as they maneuver the cube farm or the corner shop or the hospital ward or the factory floor? Is it appropriate to bring our faith with us each day?

Here's one view. It's from scholar and author Dan Boone:

[Work] is a place where divine/human encounters are played out. The tensions are remarkable. On one hand, it is a sacred partnership with God that occupies us in tending God's creation. On the other hand, it is cursed by the fall. How the same act can be gift and curse is a mystery. And our work can be done in likeness to God: creative, loving, life-embracing. Or it can be done like the devil: stealing, killing, and destroying. Work is eternal. We will be judged forever by the quality and imprint of our work. Our work follows us into tomorrow.[1]

Here's something else to think about. This comes from the late television producer Bob Briner:

It's time for believers to confidently carry their faith with them into the marketplace so that our very culture feels the difference. I'm writing to parents and ministry professionals with the prayerful hope that they will begin more intensely and systematically to teach and model the reality that every one of us is called to be a minister in our own corner of the world. I am writing with the hope that the dichotomy between professional Christians and Christians in the professions will be greatly lessened.[2]

→ **Where do you land with these two viewpoints?**
Is your job a sacred partnership with God?
Are you a minister in the workplace?

Healing Journey

At 6:00 a.m. the alarm rings.

Oh, how Josh hates to get up and go to work. It's the same thing every day: work, break, work, lunch, work, break, work, and then—ah, finally—time to go home. For him, life begins at 5:00 p.m. That's when he enjoys a meal with his girlfriend, followed by a movie—or maybe something decent on TV.

He savors these few hours of sanity. But work—"Oh, how it's a purely dreadful pursuit. But I do it for a paycheck. I do it for those few hours of sanity."

In an apartment across the hall lives Josh's neighbor Elisabeth. Her alarm goes off at 6:00 a.m., too, and she works at the same place as Josh. But Elisabeth loves what she does. She's convinced that her work is important for the success of the company. She works with enthusiasm and pride, finding personal satisfaction in every detail she completes. Evenings are fun, too, adding variety to her life.

"I have much to be thankful for," Elisabeth says with a smile. "God has blessed me with a great career—an awesome sense of purpose and fulfillment. All that I do, I approach with my whole heart, as if working for the Lord."

• • •

Two people, two jobs—yet two very different perspectives. Which one best describes you? Or to put it another way, which attitude do you demonstrate as you go about your daily tasks? As Dan Boone points out, our work "is a sacred partnership with God."

There's a big difference between working for a paycheck and working with a purpose. While having a positive attitude is an important factor here, the key ingredients are (1) discovering your God-given gifts and talents, (2) committing them to the Lord, and (3) using them to their fullest.

God has given each one of us the ability to be remarkable at something.

He wants you to find joy and satisfaction in your daily tasks. But for way too many people, "interests" and "work" are two entirely separate subjects. If all you see is the money earned and what little you can do with it, you will feel empty and unfulfilled.

Change your attitude about work. Be a cubicle missionary—confidently carrying your faith with you so that, as Bob Briner says, "our very culture feels the difference."

In the days and weeks ahead, examine carefully what you're drawn to in life—the pursuits that fascinate you. Then take the brave steps toward your dreams. And regardless of your job now—or what you end up doing in the future—if you consider work as God's gift to you, your life will become filled with gladness of heart. Begin your day praying, "God, establish the work of my hands today" (see Psalm 90:17).[3] Ask Jesus to let your light shine so others "may see your good deeds and glorify your Father in heaven" (Matthew 5:16).

Healing Steps

Don't just blend in with the masses. And don't just settle for a paycheck. Instead, stand out in the crowd and pinpoint the kind of job that gives you meaning and purpose. "Use your imagination as you think about employment possibilities," says the manager of human resources at Coca-Cola in Atlanta. "Of course, we hire people who enjoy our products."[4]

Take Christ into the workplace. In our scenario above, the biggest difference between Josh and Elisabeth does not lie in the working hand but in the attitude of the heart. Josh viewed his job as a necessary evil—a means merely to make money for the nonworking moment s of life. Elisabeth, on the other hand, found purpose and meaning within her work. She used her job to serve God and others.

Know that laziness can kill meaning, purpose, and direction. Avoid it. It can dim the focus in your work, blur the meaning in what God has called you to do. It can drain all the vitality out of your life. Ask God to remind you about the wonderful gift work really is.

Maintain a healthy attitude about knowledge, position, and self-image.

Okay, let's look into the future a bit. Let's say you've landed that prestigious position and everybody is now looking up at you. Don't let it go to your head. In fact, as your dreams become reality, you'd be wise to keep your feet firmly planted on the ground—and your head out of the clouds.

In *The Imitation of Christ*, Thomas á Kempis, author and Augustinian monk, offers some suggestions on how we should live:

> *You may know a lot, yes, but there's also a lot you don't know. "Don't be a wiseacre," wrote Paul to the Romans (11:20). Admit you're not omniscient. And when it comes to standing in line, what about the people ahead of you? Apparently, they know more than you do. Get used to knowing less than God. Get used to the middle of the line. That's where you belong.*
>
> *What's the most profound, and yet the most practical, lesson you can learn? That you look like an ant! What's the deepest wisdom and yet the highest perfection? That you are an ant! Have no illusions about yourself—that's what Paul laid on the Romans (11:20). Hold high opinions only about others.* [5]

Healing Words for Growth

Healing Words for My Family (and How I Plan to Use Them):

_____

_____

_____

_____

Healing Words for Growth:

_____

_____

_____

_____

Healing Words to Pray:

_____

_____

_____

_____

12

Unlock a Dream

To humans belong the plans of the heart, but from the Lord comes the
proper answer of the tongue. All a person's ways seem pure to them,
but motives are weighed by the Lord. Commit to the Lord whatever you
do, and he will establish your plans. The Lord works out everything to
its proper end—even the wicked for a day of disaster. The Lord detests
all the proud of heart. Be sure of this: They will not go unpunished.
Through love and faithfulness sin is atoned for; through the fear of
the Lord evil is avoided. When the Lord takes pleasure in anyone's way,
he causes their enemies to make peace with them. Better a little with
righteousness than much gain with injustice. In their hearts humans
plan their course, but the Lord establishes their steps.

PROVERBS 16:1–9

What is a dream? Is it some bizarre fantasy we have as we sleep that makes no sense when we wake in the morning? Or is it a vision of something greater pursued by great leaders such as George Washington, Martin Luther King Jr., or Mother Teresa?

These are usually the two extremes that jump into our minds when we think of dreams. What if dreams were something far more personal? What if they are the true desires of our heart? In the words of author John Eldredge, "What if those deep desires in our hearts are telling us the truth, revealing to us the life we were meant to live?"[1]

We seldom think of dreams and truth in the same thought. They are usually associated with the bizarre or the lofty. But we all have them. We call them goals, aspirations, or life plans. But these are the dreams that come from within. They are at the core of our being. We dream as differently as we are created. Even as we are influenced by our families, childhood, education, media, and relationships, we tend to return to our childhood dreams. Our desires resurface time and time again.

→ What is your dream job? How can you unlock a dream in your own life? How about in the lives of those you work with?

Healing Journey

For me (Michael), my earliest aspiration was to be a TV anchorman. I proudly announced this decision at the age of nine while standing in front of my family's pathetic little black-and-white set. (No seventy-inch flat screens in my childhood.) Our TV had a strange antenna on top called "rabbit ears" that my sister wrapped in aluminum foil, thinking it would improve the reception—which it never did.

So I'd annoy my five brothers and sisters each night, blocking the static-filled screen, lip-syncing Walter Cronkite's famous salutation, "And that's the way it is."

Our house was also down the road from our local TV station, which was essentially a tiny tin, shed-like building with much larger, more sophisticated antennas on the roof. (I think mixed in was a pair of rabbit ears.)

It was also the home of the Channel Three Eyewitness News Team.

"I'm going to be on that team one day!" I'd say every time we'd drive by and our eyes would spot the cheesy smiles of the news crew on the giant billboard that was impossible to miss. My brothers, of course, would give me a hard time, pointing out that most boys my age wanted to be firefighters and baseball stars—not TV anchormen.

Slightly embarrassed, I'd shrug my shoulders and insist, "That's who I'm going to be."

Needless to say, I never became an anchorman. God had other plans for my life. Yet the Lord has always allowed me to travel an unusual path. I believe my early proclamation was more of an insight to the type of goals I would pursue in life instead of an actual career choice.

During college, I did spend a couple of summers working in a TV newsroom—even interning with the Eyewitness team! Later I worked as a radio reporter and served as a magazine editor at Focus on the Family; and today I write books for Back to the Bible.

My hobbies include hiking, camping, painting, and international travel.

I've gone whitewater rafting in Colorado countless times—leading and ministering to fathers and their sons—and I've backpacked through the Ansel Adams wilderness in California. I'm drawn to adventure, to people and their stories, to creative pursuits. That is who God created me to be.

I'm also happily married and a proud dad. The responsibilities of being a husband and a father have proven to be the most demanding and rewarding challenges of my life.

These aren't contradictory dreams; they are just unique to me.

One of my closest friends in the world leads a completely different life. He is a project manager for a movie studio in Los Angeles and isn't into the wilderness, has no interest in writing, and prefers to travel in luxury. We appear to be complete opposites. I believe the key to our lifelong friendship is the support we have always shown each other when it comes to our dreams. We just seem to have this same basic outlook on life: We are uniquely created by God and should therefore live that way. Own it. Pursue it. Love it.

• • •

Jesus said, "I have come that they may have life, and have it to the full" (John 10:10). Are you living the life that God has chosen for you?

In the midst of responsibility and duty, we often suppress the desires of our heart. We have been created to live, love, and praise our God. Through prayer and honest self-evaluation, the desires of our heart will become clear. The pursuit of these God-given desires will draw us closer to Him and help us to define who and whose we are.

Close your eyes and imagine three desires of your heart. Don't think about them or rationalize your wishes—just dream. Does your life, in any way, represent those dreams? Are the items on your list consistent? Do you identify a theme among your wishes? How do your dreams compare to those you had as a child? When is the last time you asked God to help you clarify your dreams?

Healing Steps

Focus on the gifts and talents God has given us. Ask the Lord to reveal what His "good, pleasing and perfect will" for your life looks like (Romans 12:2).

Share dreams with others. Each day in the workplace, do you share your passion for serving Christ—and for unlocking the dreams He has placed in your heart? Do you encourage others to unlock their dreams?

> *Whatever you do, whether in word or deed, do it all in the name of the Lord Jesus, giving thanks to God the Father through him.*
> COLOSSIANS 3:17

Healing Words for Growth

Healing Words for My Family (and How I Plan to Use Them):

_____

_____

_____

_____

Healing Words for Growth:

_____

_____

_____

_____

Healing Words to Pray:

_____

_____

_____

_____

13

Secrets of a Ragamuffin Worker:
What We Can Learn from Manning and Mullins

Israel, put your hope in the LORD, for with the LORD
is unfailing love and with him is full redemption.
PSALM 130:7

One of the mysteries of the Gospel is this strange attraction of Jesus for the unattractive, this strange desire for the undesirable, this strange love for the unlovely.[1] Yet Jesus was doing exactly what the Father does: loving, forgiving, redeeming.

> *Jesus knew that the Father had put all things under his power, and that he had come from God and was returning to God; so he got up from the meal, took off his outer clothing, and wrapped a towel around his waist. After that, he poured water into a basin and began to wash his disciples' feet, drying them with the towel that was wrapped around him.*
>
> *He came to Simon Peter, who said to him, "Lord, are you going to wash my feet?"*
>
> *Jesus replied, "You do not realize now what I am doing, but later you will understand."*
>
> *"No," said Peter, "you shall never wash my feet."*
>
> *Jesus answered, "Unless I wash you, you have no part with me."*
> *(John 13:3–8)*

Jesus hung out with ragamuffins—broken, messed up, imperfect people. You and me. Here's what author Brennan Manning wrote about Christ's relentless pursuit: "The ragamuffin gospel reveals that Jesus forgives sins—including sins of the flesh—that he is comfortable with sinners who remember how to show compassion, but that he cannot and will not have a relationship with pretenders in the Spirit."[2]

→ **How do you show compassion at work?**
How do you live your faith?

Healing Journey

Rich Mullins is often described as a "master poet," a performer whose writing "bordered on brilliance." But ask anyone who knew him well, and they'll tell you he was strangely wonderful. He, like his friend Brennan Manning, described himself as a ragamuffin.

"He was definitely the most unusual guy I'd ever met," Rich's colleague and friend, musician Michael W. Smith told me (Michael). "For example, when he first moved to Nashville, he lived in a tent out in the woods. He'd also been known to hop on a motorcycle and go on long trips—like from Michigan to Alaska. He was extremely different, but I thought he was awesome. I liked him because he was very creative. He wasn't like anybody else I knew."

I couldn't agree more. Before Rich's death in 1997, I had the privilege of interviewing him on a few occasions. During our times together, I'd never quite know what to expect. Sometimes his answers to my questions would catch me off guard. (He liked doing that to people!) At other times, he'd blow my mind with a profound thought.

I liked Rich, too. But what I most admired about him was his authenticity with God and with people. Despite his obvious playful side, he wasn't into game playing when it came to spiritual matters. Rich made every effort to walk, talk, and live a real faith—"warts and all," he'd say.

In the paragraphs that follow, I've compiled some of my favorite thoughts from Rich—both from my own interviews, as well as from his conversations with others.

He had a lot to say about using healing words, especially in the workplace.

Rich on Priorities

"While I've been called strange, I've met Christians who have a warped view of what's really important in life. More people want to find out if I know Amy Grant than whether or not I know Jesus. And that's bizarre to me. Amy, like me, is a mere human in a mere mortal body, and has been given limited time on planet Earth.

"But I do know Someone who is limitless. His body won't see corruption and He has the power to raise even *me* up. I know the King of the universe, the Savior of mankind. That's a lot more impressive!"

Rich on Writing Songs

"What motivated me to write 'Awesome God'? A paycheck. I like to eat, and I need to pay the bills just like everyone else.

"Oh, wait—that's not how I'm supposed to answer that question, right? I'm supposed to say that the song grew out of my wonder for God, as well as my desire to serve Him and to see people saved. Well, of course these things are true. Of course these motives are at the core of my music—after all, my faith is who I am. But while the Lord gifted me with musical talent—I'm not canonized! Writing and performing songs is what I do to make a living.

"Now, specifically, how did 'Awesome God' come about? It was a hot summer day, and I was driving through Kansas with all my windows rolled down. I had the radio turned up, and I was listening to one of those hallelujah-style preachers. It was great! So I started yelling Bible verses at cars as they would go by me. I'm sure all the other drivers thought I was a madman! Eventually, the song 'Awesome God' came together.

"I know it's a weird story, but that's how it happened. Everybody thinks that writers sit around in this perpetual fog of inspiration. Actually, it's more of a fog of confusion."

Rich on Becoming Like Christ

"The goal is not that you should become a great Bible scholar. It's not about mere intellectual assent to a set of doctrines. The goal is that you should be like Jesus—and the scriptures can help you with that. I don't need to read the Bible because I'm a great saint. I read the Bible because I'll find God there. It's about a daily walk with this person Jesus."[3]

Rich on Serving as a Ragamuffin Worker

"Part of my motivation for moving out to the reservation, quite honestly, was that I had become very weary of twentieth-century American evangelical Christianity. I think it's okay. I don't have anything against it. I just don't think it's the whole picture. I think that putting yourself in the midst of a culture unlike the one you grew up in helps you to keep some sort of sense of balance in the way you view your faith, your life, and things going on around you.

"I still believe what marks us as Christians is not our doctrine in terms of a doctrinal statement. What marks us as Christians is our love for people. And if you love people, you respect them. No one was ever won into the kingdom through snobbery. We come to know Christ through love. I think you can profess the Apostles' Creed until Jesus returns, but if you don't love somebody you never were a Christian."[4]

Healing Steps

• *Don't be a "pretender in the Spirit."* Live your faith in true humility in the workplace—and everywhere. Take some clues from Manning and Mullins: see yourself and all Christ-followers the way the Lord sees us—as deeply loved, completely forgiven ragamuffins.

• *Communicate the ragamuffin gospel.* Share it, live it. Tell others that the death and resurrection of Jesus Christ is what frees a believer from sin, not an act of his or her own will. By faith, we daily turn our lives over to the One who has given us new life. *"And being found in appearance as a man, he humbled himself and became obedient to death—even death on a cross!" (Philippians 2:8).*

Healing Words for Growth

Healing Words for My Family (and How I Plan to Use Them):

_____

_____

_____

_____

Healing Words for Growth:

_____

_____

_____

_____

Healing Words to Pray:

_____

_____

_____

_____

14

Holding Your Tongue and Turning Your Cheek

"But to you who are listening I say: Love your enemies, do good to those
who hate you, bless those who curse you, pray for those who mistreat
you. If someone slaps you on one cheek, turn to them the other also.
If someone takes your coat, do not withhold your shirt from them.
Give to everyone who asks you, and if anyone takes what belongs to you,
do not demand it back. Do to others as you would have them do to you."
LUKE 6:27–31

Backstabbing coworkers. Angry bosses. Constant office injustices.

It's hard to handle in the workplace. Yet Christ sets the example of how we should respond: "Love your enemies, do good to those who hate you, bless those who curse you, pray for those who mistreat you."

In other words, repay others with love and humility—the opposite of pride.

And C. S. Lewis challenges us to take pride very seriously. "The essential vice, the utmost evil, is pride. Unchastity, anger, greed, drunkenness, and all that, are mere flea bites in comparison: it was through pride that the devil became the devil: Pride leads to every other vice: it is the complete anti-God state of mind."[1]

Lewis describes pride as "spiritual cancer" and warns that its presence in our lives can block us from knowing God. Have no part of it. Instead, show humility—holding your tongue and turning your cheek.

→ **What exactly are we to do to our enemies? Since applying**
verses 29–30 literally could reinforce someone's bad
behavior, what is Jesus' point (see verses 31, 36)?[2]

Healing Journey

I (Brian) am a diehard New England Patriots fan, mainly because I lived in that part of the country for most my life. Sitting in Gillette Stadium (just outside of Boston) is an unforgettable experience. The place literally buzzes with excitement. Pride runs deep with Patriots fans.

A few years back, my family and I moved to Florida, where we quickly discovered a reality about our team: we were seriously in the minority. Patriots fans were few and far between. (Obviously, most Floridians cheer for the Miami Dolphins.) And that is why I had to have a serious talk with my family *before* we ever set foot in Sun Life Stadium. Being sensitive to local fans, expressing appropriate behavior during the game, and knowing how to show our enthusiasm "when in Rome," so to speak, were the keys to avoiding a black eye.

Each family member needed to remember that cheering for the Patriots in Miami should be—and *must* be—different from the way we would show support in Foxborough, Massachusetts. The people we sat near had to be considered carefully as we measured our outward enthusiasm. Even the flow and the score of the game needed to be considered.

In all honesty, this type of lesson applies to many other life experiences. We need to measure our setting before we execute our communication. Proverbs 25:11 (ESV) says, "A word fitly spoken is like apples of gold in a setting of silver." The right circumstances can make or break the same words.

I am an early morning person and wake up alert before anyone in my family. As it is in most households, certain people are morning people while others don't fully wake up until evening. This is true for our family as well, and one thing this means is that my morning greeting should be different for different people. Those who wake up early and alert are ready for dialogue and interaction. Those who are slower to wake up need softer voices and less interaction. Some people may need extra space and no interaction!

What are the factors that play into the right circumstances so that our words are best received? Here are three considerations:
- The right time
- The right place
- The right people.

You may believe that a person who has had a very difficult week just needs an enthusiastic word from you to turn the corner and become joyful. That may be the case, but it would be prudent to understand their circumstances before engaging them in any meaningful way. What does it look like to be prudent when it comes to speech? Again, Proverbs gives us wisdom in 10:19: "Sin is not ended by multiplying words, but the prudent hold their tongues."

Cautious speech often results in fewer words being shared. This is more than "Think before you speak." This is more like "Think, do your due diligence, then speak."

Healing Steps

Nurture the opposite of pride in your speech: humility, love, contentment, common sense.

Don't delay in getting to the root of sin. Ask God to examine your heart. If pride is present, pray for healing. Ask Him to remove this form of spiritual cancer. Ask God to help you live His teaching in Luke 6:27–31.

Ask Christ to help you repay the unkindness of others with the love of God. "Don't have anything to do with foolish and stupid arguments, because you know they produce quarrels. And the Lord's servant must not be quarrelsome but must be kind to everyone, able to teach, not resentful. Opponents must be gently instructed, in the hope that God will grant them repentance leading them to a knowledge of the truth, and that they will come to their senses and escape from the trap of the devil, who has taken them captive to do his will" (2 Timothy 2:23–26).

Healing Words for Growth

Healing Words for My Family (and How I Plan to Use Them):

_____

_____

_____

_____

Healing Words for Growth:

_____

_____

_____

_____

Healing Words to Pray:

_____

_____

_____

_____

15

"But I Feel Like a Christian Doormat" (When and How to Speak Up)

When the LORD takes pleasure in anyone's way,
he causes their enemies to make peace with them.
PROVERBS 16:7

The Lord tells us—from the beginning of the Bible to the end—that He has conquered fear and has overcome the trials and tribulations of this world. We are no longer slaves to them. As His children we are free!

Know what else? We are not Christian doormats—at home, at church, in our communities, or at work. And we don't have to live like one.

If you find yourself facing a seemingly insurmountable struggle at work and are beginning to feel paralyzed by fear and frustration, here's what you should do: (1) surrender your emotions and your trials to God in prayer, (2) take some steps toward change with the Lord's guidance, and then (3) brace yourself. The battle may get nasty before it gets better. But if you're on the side of truth, hold on to hope. God has your back.

"When the light comes the darkness must depart," explained nineteenth-century preacher Charles H. Spurgeon. "Where truth is, the lie must flee. If the lie remains, there will be a severe conflict, because truth cannot and will not lower its standard. If you follow Christ, all the hounds of the world will yelp at your heels."[1]

→ **Have you mistakenly believed that it is okay to be manipulated because you're a Christian? Explain your answer. When and how should you speak up?**

Healing Journey

Radio talk show host and author Paul Coughlin knows what it's like to feel like a Christian doormat. Take a look at a pivotal point in his career when he decided, "Enough is enough!" This following excerpt is from his book *No More Christian Nice Guy*.

> *I had a boss tell me and my coworkers during workplace "Bible studies" about his biblical covering in our lives. Wouldn't you know it, many if not most of those studies ended with admonishment to obey the authority figures in our life, to work hard as working unto the Lord, and related directives. They were good and right messages, but they were hollow and self-serving coming from him. Oh, the madness we Christian nice guys (CNGs) have tolerated in the name of being nice Christians.*
>
> *Again, since this supposed covering is an extra-biblical revelation, the person who speaks it into being gets to define what it means. My boss, whom I should not have mistaken as a leader, told me that I was to put myself under his teaching the same way I was supposed to follow and not question my pastor. He was part of the biblical authority structure in my life now, and if I didn't obey him, then he might withhold his "blessing" in my life the way God, he said, withholds his blessing from those who disobey.*
>
> *Such teaching was in line with the doctrine put forward by the heavy-handed church I attended at the time. I "submitted" myself to his authority, and my, the stories I could tell.*
>
> *I eventually wised up and found another job. (Nice Guys: Don't tell people you're looking for another job. Just do it, and not because you're afraid of being fired, but because you want to preserve your integrity.) When I told my boss, he said he was withholding his God-powered blessing. The words I then uttered aided my climb out of the CNG hole: "I don't want your 'blessing.' It doesn't exist."*
>
> *Christian Nice Guys are fodder for such manipulation; they need the strong people in our churches to defend them against this nonsense, because this isn't even close to the worst of such ideas. Some CNGs even come to believe that not only are they to seek their boss's "blessing," a kiss*

*of death for a passive person. . .[but that] your workplace loyalty is to
God and to the gifts he's given you. And if you're married, your loyalties
also include your wife, and kids if you have them. You never swore an
allegiance to your boss, and you were never required to do so; just don't
put it past the male-diminishing church to try to create one.*[2]

Healing Steps

Don't just "roll over and play dead." If your workplace circumstances have
gotten to the point of becoming unbearable, remind yourself of two things:
(1) you have choices, and (2) your suffering *will* end. You may think you
don't deserve good treatment at work, and so you put a Christian veneer on
it by mistaking your workplace suffering with suffering for the Gospel's sake.
That's a mistake. "You are free to do in the workplace what's best for you and
your family," writes Paul Coughlin. "God put a beat in you—certain abilities,
desires, and attributes. Come out of your hiding place and dance to it."[3]

Accept that challenges are a part of life—and work (John 16:33). Even if
you fix your problems at work and circumstances are peaceful right now,
brace yourself: another storm is on the horizon. Living in a sad, sinful world
involves pain—it's part of the program. So decide under whose hand you'll
suffer. God's or Satan's? Satan is a torturer. He makes sure sin tastes good on
the first bite, but there's always a razor blade in the apple. In contrast, God is
a healer. He uses inevitable pain in your life to strengthen you, mixing true
joy and contentment with your suffering. It's your choice. Choose well.

Remind yourself that suffering brings you close to Jesus (Philippians 3:10).
In suffering for Him, you'll appreciate His great sufferings for you. And in
your every struggle, He suffers with you. What's more, He gives you the
strength to endure: "For the grace of God has appeared that offers salvation
to all people. It teaches us to say 'No' to ungodliness and worldly passions,
and to live self-controlled, upright and godly lives in this present age, while
we wait for the blessed hope—the appearing of the glory of our great God
and Savior, Jesus Christ, who gave himself for us to redeem us from all
wickedness and to purify for himself a people that are his very own, eager to
do what is good" (Titus 2:11–14).[4]

Healing Words for Growth

Healing Words for My Family (and How I Plan to Use Them):

_____

_____

_____

_____

Healing Words for Growth:

_____

_____

_____

_____

Healing Words to Pray:

_____

_____

_____

_____

16

Shared Meaning: A Transformational Communication Style

My dear brothers and sisters, take note of this:
Everyone should be quick to listen, slow to speak and slow to become angry.
JAMES 1:19

Communication takes two people: a sender and a receiver. Yet when there's *static* in the communication process, friction arises, and no one is able to connect. What kinds of static? Defensiveness, misunderstandings, preconceived notions, hurt feelings, misplaced anger.

Sound familiar?

It happens at home, at church, in our communities. . .and most certainly in the workplace. Up to this point, our conversation has focused on ways of being a Christ-follower on the job, as well as on tips for sharing words that heal. This chapter offers a plan that guarantees you will be heard.

→ **What sparks conflicts at work?**
How do you and your coworkers resolve them?

Healing Journey
Conversation #1—How It Could Be

Your Coworker: "I have some serious concerns about this report, and I can't believe you were about to send it to the district sales manager. It's full of typos, and some of last year's stats are way off. What were you thinking?"

You: "Thanks for bringing this to my attention. Do you mind taking a seat and showing me your concerns—especially where you feel I went wrong? I want to get this right, so I really appreciate your help."

Your Coworker: "Yeah, I guess so. I'm pretty busy right now, but this is important. I'll adjust my schedule and will take some time to review this with you. Let's meet in your office in fifteen minutes."

You: "Perfect! I can't thank you enough for helping out."

Your Coworker: "No problem. That's why we're on the same team, right? We have each other's backs."

Conversation #2—How It Usually Is

Your Coworker: "I have some serious concerns about this report, and I can't believe you were about to send it to the district sales manager. It's full of typos, and some of last year's stats are way off. What were you thinking?"

You: "Wow! There you go again—the office complainer. What's your problem? Wake up on the wrong side of the bed again? Look—I'm not perfect, so sue me!"

Your Coworker: "You never listen to me, especially when I'm trying to save your tail. You need to stop being so hardheaded and realize that I'm here to help you."

You: "Help me? Or make me look bad? I wish you'd stop trying to stick your nose in my business."

Your Coworker: "I'm really getting tired of these stupid arguments. Why do I even try? Fine, look like the company fool. See if I care."

• • •

So which conversation is more common with your coworkers? If it's the second one, that's too bad, because Conversation #1 isn't that far out of touch with reality. In fact, with some work, it can actually be the regular mode of conversation in the workplace. But it all begins with an important nine-letter word: *listening*.

Countless conflicts could be avoided—or at least better managed—if two people would lower their defenses and strive to hear each other. These healing steps can help.

Healing Steps

Listening is where effective communication really begins. Instead of engaging in a verbal tug-of-war with people you work with, try the following.[1]

Begin with passive listening (or silence). Give the other person a chance to speak his mind. For instance, he might say, "I'm just not understanding your memos. They are a little long, and sometimes the important action points and project parameters are buried in the middle, making them easy to miss."

Give acknowledgment responses. Don't just stand there with a blank expression on your face. Even when you're listening passively, it's a good idea to make sincere comments, such as "I see" or "Oh?" that emphasize that you are paying attention.

Offer a "door opener." This is a simple, nonjudgmental statement, such as, "How would you feel if I asked the office manager to proof your reports before they are sent out? Maybe he can offer some light editing, as well." How-you-feel questions are less threatening to others, and they help spark communication.

Exercise active listening with a communication style called "shared meaning." Here's how it works:

- You're frustrated because an important company report is substandard, and a teammate in your department (the person who authored it) didn't even bother to involve you; he just placed it on the office manager's desk with the instructions to "copy and send out." So you approach him and say, "We need to talk about this. I have some concerns."

- Once you have his attention, you explain your point of view (which you've thought through ahead of time) without being interrupted.

- Next, your coworker repeats what he heard you say.
- You then clarify or confirm what he said, ensuring that your thoughts and feelings have been heard accurately.
- The process continues with him sharing his point of view and you listening and repeating what he said.

The goal of shared meaning is to be heard accurately. And once you've had a chance to state your case and listen to that of another person, the foundation is set for communication and for a fair solution to the problem at hand—a solution that's grounded on listening and being heard, not just another pointless workplace conflict.

Healing Words for Growth

Healing Words for My Family (and How I Plan to Use Them):

_____

_____

_____

_____

Healing Words for Growth:

_____

_____

_____

_____

Healing Words to Pray:

_____

_____

_____

_____

17

Ten Basics of Workplace Evangelism

In your hearts revere Christ as Lord. Always be prepared to give an
answer to everyone who asks you to give the reason for the hope
that you have. But do this with gentleness and respect, keeping a
clear conscience, so that those who speak maliciously against your
good behavior in Christ may be ashamed of their slander.
1 PETER 3:15–16

When it comes to communicating the greatest news of all—eternal freedom through Jesus Christ—most of us feel clueless, speechless, and completely ineffective. Yet in spite of how inadequate we feel, Christ has given each of His followers an essential mission: "We are. . .Christ's ambassadors, as though God were making his appeal through us" (2 Corinthians 5:20). In this passage we are instructed to be ready with answers—instead of just being polite and keeping quiet.

Perhaps some of your coworkers don't seem very interested in spiritual issues right now, but they're watching you—especially your faith. And if they come to you with a question one day, you need to speak up.

> → **Are you able to verbalize what you believe?**
> **(Why or why not?) Share three key ways**
> **that Jesus Christ has changed your life.**

Healing Journey

Amy scrunches into a tiny ball on the couch in the break room and rests her chin on her knee. The conversation between two other coworkers is almost too much to handle.

"Are you sure, Sarah?" Danielle presses. "I mean, you could be a little late because of your training for the marathon, stress—stuff like that."

"Look, I'm not just a little late. Trust me, I know what's happening inside my own body." Sarah puts her hand on her stomach and looks down. "I'm about fourteen weeks along."

"Have you told your husband?" Danielle asks.

"Are you kidding? He'll know it isn't his. . .considering that we don't even sleep in the same bed lately."

"How about. . .him?" Danielle adds, looking in the direction of another colleague's office. (It was no secret that Sarah wasn't being faithful to her husband.)

Sarah shakes her head no.

A stabbing pain shoots through Amy's stomach as she listens. She just can't imagine facing such a hard dilemma. Yes, as a Christian, Amy knows that Christ is the solution to any problem in life. But how can she express this to her hurting coworker?

Amy leans back and squeezes her eyes shut. *Lord, I know that I should speak up, but I don't know what to say—or even where to begin. How can I help?*

• • •

Life is messy, and sin is painful. Actually, it's deadly. Amy needs to speak up and offer her friends the hope of Jesus Christ. Yet who can blame her for feeling nervous?

The truth is, sharing our faith should be the most natural thing in the world, because it's really nothing more than telling someone else the story of what God has done for us. When we talk about Jesus, we are sharing our faith. When we tell the story of our spiritual journey in front of a group, we are sharing our faith. When we tell people about Jesus in a letter or e-mail message, we are sharing our faith. So how about the places we go to earn a living?

Following are ten basics of workplace evangelism.

Healing Steps

1. *Witness with words.* You don't have to hand out tracts to share your faith in Christ, but you can drop signals—low-key or boldly, whatever you're comfortable with—to let them know where you stand. Incorporate

your faith naturally into your everyday conversations. (For tips, flip over to chapter 36: "Three Stories: A Way to Witness.") "I am not ashamed of the gospel, because it is the power of God that brings salvation to everyone who believes: first to the Jew, then to the Gentile" (Romans 1:16).

2. *Witness without words.* Let others see Christ through your lifestyle. Strive to be kind and trustworthy. Be a good employee and work with excellence. "Slaves, obey your earthly masters in everything; and do it, not only when their eye is on you and to win their favor, but with sincerity of heart and reverence for the Lord" (Colossians 3:22).

3. *Witness with creativity.* Does your church host concerts, plays, craft fairs, or family adventure camps? Invite people from the workplace to join you. "For we are God's handiwork, created in Christ Jesus to do good works, which God prepared in advance for us to do" (Ephesians 2:10).

4. *Be real (and realistic).* Face it, Christ-followers aren't perfect. We're human! Don't be defensive if you mess up at work, and never try to hide your mistakes. Own up to them. Your coworkers will be drawn to someone who is real. "Therefore if you have any encouragement from being united with Christ, if any comfort from his love, if any common sharing in the Spirit, if any tenderness and compassion, then make my joy complete by being like-minded, having the same love, being one in spirit and of one mind. Do nothing out of selfish ambition or vain conceit. Rather, in humility value others above yourselves, not looking to your own interests but each of you to the interests of the others" (Philippians 2:1–4).

5. *Be ready.* The Bible tells us to "keep watch" and to "be ready" with an answer about your faith. (For tips, flip over to chapter 38: "Powerful Words That Open Doors.") "Therefore keep watch, because you do not know on what day your Lord will come" (Matthew 24:42).

6. *Be respectful.* If you sense that someone has no interest in visiting your church or hearing about your faith, back off. Give them space, be respectful, but continue to witness *without* words. "Give to everyone what you owe them: If you owe taxes, pay taxes; if revenue, then revenue; if respect, then respect; if honor, then honor" (Romans 13:7).

7. *Don't be confrontational.* Definitely stand up for what you believe,

but remember that yelling and Bible thumping won't win souls. A better approach: direct people to God's Word and allow scripture to quietly convict them. "All Scripture is breathed out by God and profitable for teaching, for reproof, for correction, and for training in righteousness" (2 Timothy 3:16 ESV).

8. *Don't be a Christian "know-it-all."* As C. S. Lewis observed, "If I may trust my personal experience, no doctrine is, for the moment, dimmer to the eye of faith than that which a man has just successfully defended."[1] Your coworkers will respond less to head knowledge and more to love. "If I speak in the tongues of men or of angels, but do not have love, I am only a resounding gong or a clanging cymbal" (1 Corinthians 13:1)

9. *Speak kindly about others.* Try to find something positive to say about everyone at work—even the most cantankerous colleague. "Be kind to one another, tenderhearted, forgiving one another, as God in Christ forgave you" (Ephesians 4:32 ESV).

10. *Speak kindly about your boss.* Joining in on a gripe session about the injustices of management may feel like a good way to score points with your coworkers, but don't do it. It will eventually come back to bite you. (Trust us on this point.) Choose to be different. Choose to be above bad-mouthing your boss. Show that you are trustworthy, not a backstabber. "Remind the people to be subject to rulers and authorities, to be obedient, to be ready to do whatever is good, to slander no one, to be peaceable and considerate, and always to be gentle toward everyone" (Titus 3:1–2).

Healing Words for Growth

Healing Words for My Family (and How I Plan to Use Them):

Healing Words for Growth:

_____

_____

_____

_____

Healing Words to Pray:

_____

_____

_____

_____

18

Kind Words for Mean Bosses

*Sometimes we do what is right and suffer for it. Job's friends all
had PhDs in wisdom but were declared by God to be dead wrong.
Suffice it to say, there is no divine guarantee that if we do the right
things we will get the results we want. There is rogue suffering in our
world, and sometimes our vocation finds us right in the middle of it.*
DAN BOONE[1]

"I Will Honor Your Position"

1 Peter 2:13–17: "Submit yourselves for the Lord's sake to every human
authority: whether to the emperor, as the supreme authority, or to governors,
who are sent by him to punish those who do wrong and to commend those
who do right. For it is God's will that by doing good you should silence
the ignorant talk of foolish people. Live as free people, but do not use your
freedom as a cover-up for evil; live as God's slaves. Show proper respect to
everyone, love the family of believers, fear God, honor the emperor."

How to Endure: What does the apostle Peter mean when he says to
"submit yourselves"? How should we submit ourselves to a mean boss?
Verses 15–17 offer us some clues: (1) *do good*, (2) *live as God's slaves*, (3)
show proper respect, (4) *honor the emperor*. In other words, *choose* to take
the high road and to do what's right. *Choose* to have a good attitude
and to model godly behavior—even when our good behavior is not
reciprocated.

"I Will Respect Your Authority"

1 Peter 2:18–19: "Slaves, in reverent fear of God submit yourselves to
your masters, not only to those who are good and considerate, but also to
those who are harsh. For it is commendable if someone bears up under the
pain of unjust suffering because they are conscious of God."

How to Endure: Even though you are under the authority of your boss, it doesn't mean you are a "doormat"; nor does it mean that you are, in fact, an actual "slave" to your job. You deserve the dignity that's intrinsic to being made in God's image. Therefore, we suggest that you go to your superior and respectfully discuss a situation in which you've been wronged. But if it becomes pretty obvious that your words are bouncing off a brick wall—and ultimately smacking you in the face—consider doing what verses 18–19 suggest. Take your problem to Christ, our righteous Judge, and ask for His strength to endure. And in the days and weeks that follow, make sure your boss knows that you respect his or her authority in spite of the fact that you dislike your treatment.

"I Will Submit to Your Leadership"

1 Peter 2:20–25: "But how is it to your credit if you receive a beating for doing wrong and endure it? But if you suffer for doing good and you endure it, this is commendable before God. To this you were called, because Christ suffered for you, leaving you an example, that you should follow in his steps. 'He committed no sin, and no deceit was found in his mouth.' When they hurled their insults at him, he did not retaliate; when he suffered, he made no threats. Instead, he entrusted himself to him who judges justly. 'He himself bore our sins' in his body on the cross, so that we might die to sins and live for righteousness; 'by his wounds you have been healed.' For 'you were like sheep going astray,' but now you have returned to the Shepherd and Overseer of your souls."

How to Endure: Examine closely what Peter is expressing in this passage, especially these two thoughts: (1) "But if you suffer for doing good and you endure it, this is commendable before God" (verse 20), and (2) "by his wounds you have been healed" (verse 24). What is your reaction? Why is this kind of suffering *commendable* before God? Are you encouraged—or do comments like "To this you were called" (verse 21) leave you stressed and confused? If stress is taking a toll, find healing in the remainder of this verse: "Christ suffered for you, leaving you an example, that you should follow in his steps." Here's something we highly recommend: seek out a trustworthy *confidant*—someone who can help you navigate a difficult situation at work. Whether you choose your spouse, a pastor, or a best friend, you need someone you feel comfortable opening up to and sharing what you are going through, someone who will listen.

Christ-Followers, Plant These Words and Grow

Nourish spiritual growth with God's Word. Regardless of our circumstances, our workplace loyalty is to Jesus. We need to commit our abilities to Him and to maintain a God-honoring testimony—even around the meanest of bosses. The key? Remember who you belong to: "God, being rich in mercy, because of the great love with which he loved us, even when we were dead in our trespasses, made us alive together with Christ—by grace you have been saved—and raised us up with him and seated us with him in the heavenly places in Christ Jesus, so that in the coming ages he might show the immeasurable riches of his grace in kindness toward us in Christ Jesus. For by grace you have been saved through faith. And this is not your own doing; it is the gift of God" (Ephesians 2:4–9 ESV).

Author and Christian scholar Dan Boone reminds us that there is rogue suffering in the world, including in the workplace. He suggests that instead of praying for deliverance from these hard places, we should ask God for the courage to be His person in the middle of them. "What if our deepest fellowship with God is sharing in the suffering of Christ where we work, in hope of resurrection to a new way in the workplace?" Dan writes. "What if we prayed for wisdom to respond to evil boldly, for strength from the Spirit to endure, and for tact to act rightly for the sake of all involved?. . . I am not suggesting that we are the messiah for everything broken or that Monday morning we give the boss a piece of our mind about his lousy ethics. I am suggesting that our work with God affords us wisdom from the scriptures, friends in the faith, and guidance from prayers to know how and when to respond to evil in the workplace."[2]

In the days ahead, do the following:

Plot a course for growth. List your goals:
In one month I want to. . .
In six months I want to. . .
In one year I want to. . .

List ten steps that you will take to grow (and reach your goals above):

1. _____
2. _____
3. _____
4. _____
5. _____
6. _____
7. _____
8. _____
9. _____
10. _____

19

Kind Words for Cantankerous Colleagues

*Bad work environments can get your creative juices flowing
like few other experiences. . . . Some of the best ideas and creative
results can rise from the blues in the workplace. Many meaningful
endeavors have been launched while in the throes of vocational pain,
and many worthy undertakings wouldn't have been launched if
it weren't for the thorny ground of difficulty. Take comfort from this;
good can and does come from bad.*

PAUL COUGHLIN[1]

"I'll Give You My Blessing in Spite of. . ."

Luke 6:27–31 (ESV): "But I say to you who hear, Love your enemies, do good to those who hate you, bless those who curse you, pray for those who abuse you. To one who strikes you on the cheek, offer the other also, and from one who takes away your cloak do not withhold your tunic either. Give to everyone who begs from you, and from one who takes away your goods do not demand them back. And as you wish that others would do to you, do so to them."

How to Endure: Heartless dictators and namby-pamby wimps, spineless yes-men and exhausting Eeyores, complainers, pessimists, and know-it-alls—what do these personality types have in common? They represent people you know—the men and women you work with, those you see at church, and the individuals you depend on. They're even the people you live with. So how can you possibly coexist with a less-than-enjoyable personality? Luke—Paul's friend and coworker and the presumed author of the third Gospel—instructs us to live generously the *servant* life. In other words, instead of being focused on *me* and getting *my* way, we strive to respect the uniqueness of others and to find common ground with them. Here's how *The Message* presents Luke's advice: "Love your enemies. Let them bring out the best in you, not the worst. When someone gives you a hard time, respond with the energies of prayer for that person. If someone slaps you in the face, stand there and take it. If someone grabs your shirt, giftwrap your best coat and make a present of it. If someone takes unfair advantage of you, use the occasion to practice the servant life. No more tit-for-tat stuff. Live generously."

"I Care about Everyone at This Workplace"

Romans 12:9–21: "Love must be sincere. Hate what is evil; cling to what is good. Be devoted to one another in love. Honor one another above yourselves. Never be lacking in zeal, but keep your spiritual fervor, serving the Lord. Be joyful in hope, patient in affliction, faithful in prayer. Share with the Lord's people who are in need. Practice hospitality.

"Bless those who persecute you; bless and do not curse. Rejoice with those who rejoice; mourn with those who mourn. Live in harmony with one another. Do not be proud, but be willing to associate with people of low position. Do not be conceited.

"Do not repay anyone evil for evil. Be careful to do what is right in the eyes of everyone. If it is possible, as far as it depends on you, live at peace with everyone. Do not take revenge, my dear friends, but leave room for God's wrath, for it is written: 'It is mine to avenge; I will repay,' says the Lord. On the contrary: 'If your enemy is hungry, feed him; if he is thirsty, give him something to drink. In doing this, you will heap burning coals on his head.' Do not be overcome by evil, but overcome evil with good."

How to Endure: As you consider what Paul is expressing in this passage, address some key questions: (1) Of the commands listed in these verses, which ones are the easiest and which ones are the hardest to keep? (2) Think about a specific workplace relationship. What can you do to begin living in harmony with that person? Spend some time in prayer, asking Jesus to show you how to "keep your spiritual fervor," to continue to serve Him when others are sour, to be joyful in hope, and—above all—patient in affliction.

"Here's a Peace Offering"

2 Timothy 2:23–26: "Don't have anything to do with foolish and stupid arguments, because you know they produce quarrels. And the Lord's servant must not be quarrelsome but must be kind to everyone, able to teach, not resentful. Opponents must be gently instructed, in the hope that God will grant them repentance leading them to a knowledge of the truth, and that they will come to their senses and escape from the trap of the devil, who has taken them captive to do his will."

How to Endure: What do you need to pursue in the workplace: Righteousness? Faith? Love? Peace? In what specific ways can you present a peace offering to a cantankerous colleague? Verses 25–26 may offer some clues: "Opponents must be gently instructed, in the hope that God will grant them repentance leading them to a knowledge of the truth, and that they will come to their senses and escape from the trap of the devil, who has taken them captive to do his will." Pick an appropriate time and connect with a difficult colleague. Try to find some common ground and to see eye to eye. Spend time praying for him or her before you meet.

Christ-Followers, Plant These Words and Grow

Nourish spiritual growth with God's Word. The secret to handling cantankerous people, according to Proverbs 15:1–7, rests in a gentle answer and a healing tongue: "A gentle answer turns away wrath, but a harsh word stirs up anger. The tongue of the wise adorns knowledge, but the mouth of the fool gushes folly. The eyes of the LORD are everywhere, keeping watch on the wicked and the good. The soothing tongue is a tree of life, but a perverse tongue crushes the spirit. A fool spurns a parent's discipline, but whoever heeds correction shows prudence. The house of the righteous contains great treasure, but the income of the wicked brings ruin. The lips of the wise spread knowledge, but the hearts of fools are not upright."

Yet as you seek peace, don't be completely discouraged by a challenging work environment. Author and radio talk show host Paul Coughlin is convinced that some of the best ideas and creative results can rise from the blues in the workplace. He warns, however, that Christians should be *smart*, not namby-pamby pushovers. "I believe in sacrifice in the workplace," he writes. "Just make sure it's a real sacrifice. Here's what I mean: It's a virtue to lay down your rights for the love of another. It's foolish and destructive to lay down your rights in the workplace because you fear what will happen if you don't. This is what you're doing. . .and others see it. It's no Christian witness to be walked on because you're passive."[2]

In the days ahead, do the following:

Plot a course for growth. List your goals:
In one month I want to. . .
In six months I want to. . .
In one year I want to. . .

List ten steps that you will take to grow (and reach your goals above):

1. _____
2. _____
3. _____
4. _____
5. _____
6. _____
7. _____
8. _____
9. _____
10. _____

20

Ready to Rethink the Workplace and Start Walking Our Witness?

Being a roaring lamb. . .is about everyday people doing everyday jobs with a very special goal—that of effectively representing Christ in all areas of society. Our churches should exist for this.

BOB BRINER[1]

Chart a Healing Path toward Change

1. *Receive God's Word.* Read or listen to Colossians 3:18–25.

2. *Reflect on verses 23–24.* Pull them apart word by word, looking for God's personal message to you. Invite the Holy Spirit to speak to you.

Whatever you do, work at it with all your heart, as working for the Lord, not for human masters, since you know that you will receive an inheritance from the Lord as a reward. It is the Lord Christ you are serving.

3. *Engage in a conversation with God.* After a moment of silence before the Lord, write out a dialogue between you and Him. Begin with general thoughts and impressions.

Heavenly Father, here's how I feel about these verses:

_____

_____

_____

_____

Here's what's hard for me, God—what I don't understand how to apply to my life:

_____

_____

_____

_____

Now relate these verses to your specific circumstances.

Here's what Colossians 3:18–25 is telling me about how You want me to view my work and those I work with:

_____

_____

_____

_____

With your help, Lord, here's how I'll try to represent You in my workplace:

_____

_____

_____

_____

4. *Memorize Colossians 3:24–25* and repeat it to yourself as often as needed. Write it on an index card and post it within sight.

It is the Lord Christ you are serving. Anyone who does wrong will be repaid for their wrongs, and there is no favoritism.

5. *Respond to God's nudges.* Try our *Change Your Workplace Perspective* exercise. Face it, representing Christ in the workplace isn't easy. Constantly having to endure a mean boss or turn the other cheek for that cantankerous colleague is stressful. Yet God calls believers to take the high road by extending compassion, empathy, and forgiveness to everyone—even unkind people. So what's the answer to coping, and even finding joy, in a less-than-perfect environment? Try these steps:

- *Begin by reminding yourself that there's a deeper reason why each of us behaves the way we behave.* Countless reasons: insecurity, jealousy, envy, fear, stress—the list goes on and on. Simply put, hurt people *hurt* people.
- *Next, take some time to look inward and assess your own behaviors and attitudes.* As you study the chart below, prayerfully consider two things about yourself: (1) the traps you have fallen into at work, and (2) how the truth of God can set you free, helping you to be a servant—not a victim.[2] Record your thoughts below.

Change Your Workplace Perspective

Workplace Trap	Wrong Thinking	Resulting Struggle
Performance Trap	I must succeed and meet certain standards in order to be worthy.	Fear of failure; perfectionism; driven to succeed.
Approval Trap	I must gain the approval of others in order to be worthy.	Fear of rejection; being a people pleaser; overly sensitive to criticism.
Blame Trap	Those who fail (including myself) are unworthy and deserve rejection.	Fear of rejection; Blaming others for personal failures; driven to avoid failure.

Performance Trap: _____

My Healing Path: _____

Approval Trap: _____

My Healing Path: _____

Blame Trap: _____

My Healing Path: _____

Right Thinking	Healing Path
God has forgiven me through Jesus Christ (justification). I am fully pleasing to the Father (Rom. 5:1).	I am valuable just as I am. I do not have to perform or live by impossible standards.
God has brought me into an intimate relationship with Him through Christ (reconciliation). I am totally accepted by God (Col. 1:21–22).	I am accepted just as I am. My self-worth isn't based on what others think of me.
God's wrath has been satisfied through Christ's death on the cross (propitiation). I am deeply loved by God (1 John 4:9–11).	I am loved just as I am. Even if I fail, I am not condemned.

By assessing my own behaviors and attitudes—in particular, the comments and actions of others that seem to push my buttons—here's how I can become more confident and learn to handle less-than-perfect circumstances at work:

_____

_____

_____

_____

By extending compassion and empathy—especially by reminding myself that "hurt people hurt people"—here's how I can do a better job of walking my witness and reaching out to my colleagues in the workplace:

_____

_____

_____

_____

Part Three

HEALING WORDS FOR THE FAMILY

21

Building a Stress-Less Home

Whoever walks in integrity walks securely,
but whoever takes crooked paths will be found out.
PROVERBS 10:9

It's a bit unnerving and definitely humbling, yet it's a reality of parenting: our children are watching us. And during their early years, their brains are like sponges, soaking up our words, our emotions, and our behaviors.

So what are we *really* teaching them?

They learn how to be Christians as they pattern their lives after ours—just as boys learn how to be husbands and fathers by what they see us do and little girls learn how to be wives and mothers in the same way. They observe and often absorb our attitudes and imitate our communication styles. By the time they launch into adulthood, our kids' core beliefs about faith, life, and relationships often resemble ours.

Note the word *often*, however. Despite our best efforts and the hope we have in Proverbs 22:6 ("Start children off on the way they should go, and even when they are old they will not turn from it"), some adult children reject their parents' values. (More on this in the next chapter.) Still, here's what I (Michael) have observed in most households: children learn how to worry—*from us*.

And like it or not, they are becoming increasingly anxious.

→ How would you describe your family?
Stressed-out, peaceful—bouncing between the two?
Explain your answer. If you and your loved ones
are anxious, what steps can you take to stress less?

Healing Journey

Exhausted—again.

Today isn't any different than any other random day of Tiffany's life. The alarm began its annoying buzzing at 6:30 a.m., and she started her morning stretching routine to make it shut up. Every nine minutes her arm sneaked out of the warm covers and hit her alarm clock—which is also her cell phone.

Of course it is. Why would she sleep more than three feet away from her lifeline? This young mom needs something to do at 2:34 a.m. when she's wide awake. She can return email, check the weather, send a birthday text, add items to her shopping list, take notes for the novel she's been working on for more than three years, review her prayer list, search for her dream vacation, transfer money between accounts, or even play a round of mahjong (her favorite game). Tiffany usually stops when her wrists begin to ache from what she is sure is a near-future case of carpel tunnel syndrome.

If she's still awake, she can always get up and fold laundry or unload and reload the dishwasher. But she usually lies there frustrated because she can't sleep. Tiffany finally gets around to talking to God, though her prayer usually begins with "Why can't I sleep?"

But then she finds herself remembering how amazing God is and how blessed she is. After several minutes of praise and reflection, Tiffany usually falls back into a deep slumber. So she shouldn't be surprised when she stretches out her arm to hit the snooze! Then she jumps to her feet in panic. *Oh no, I've over slept again.* She quickly starts deleting chores off of her to-do list so she can make it out the door in time. *Microwave breakfast, skip washing my hair, throw on some clean clothes (just folded at 4:00 a.m.), turn the ringer to the ON position, clean the snow off of the car, and head out for the day.*

And Tiffany's day is no different than her nights. She guzzles caffeine and snacks on power foods as she multitasks her way through the day. She sends out detailed status reports at work. She hits the gym several times a week. She compares prices and finds the best deal in town before she shops. She volunteers at church. She invests a lot of time and energy landscaping her front yard. She goes to lunch with friends. She gets the oil changed in her car every three thousand miles. She takes the cats to the vet. She does it all! She tries to slow down, but she just feels guilty.

Why would I do less than I'm capable of?

She works so hard trying to achieve the life she wants—the one she feels she deserves from all the hard work. But lately she has been wondering if it's what she's supposed to be working toward. She often feels burned-out, stressed-out, and on a treadmill of never-ending worry. *Something's wrong with this picture.*

Tiffany's early morning conversations with God have been leading her to reexamine her goals. *Could my life be different? Should it be? I know the life of a believer is supposed to be better, more peaceful, surrendered to God—more fulfilling. But what does that mean?*[1]

• • •

Do these scenarios sound like your typical day—and night? The current reality in America, regardless of age or family structure, is that we're over-extended. And at times it seems there isn't a calendar big enough to hold all that we have planned.

When we—our research department at Back to the Bible—first began talking to people about their spiritual lives, a common theme was that they felt "too busy" to spend time with God between Sundays. In fact, it seems that much of our day is spent trying to make our hectic lives work *without* God in the center. Yes, we may say a quick prayer before we rush out the door in the morning or as we're falling into bed at night, but during the in-between hours we keep God in a box.

Tweens are echoing a desire to slow their lives down a bit, too. Laura, a quiet, blue-eyed twelve-year-old, said that busyness makes it hard for her to follow Jesus: "With clarinet, piano, and Girl Scouts, I have something almost every day after school. Sometimes I don't even think about God unless I'm in church." Surprisingly, a slower pace in Sunday school was one way tweens said life could be improved. More than another game, a fun craft, or tastier snacks, they want time to really ask questions and have conversations with their teachers about what's going on in their lives.

Rushing from activity to activity crowds God from our lives. Yet we still expect Him to cooperate with us—relating to us on *our* terms, revolving around *our* plans, solving problems so we can live the way *we* want to live.

Other consequences come from not allowing any margins. We can see it when something unexpected throws a wrench into the works. What happens when turmoil hits? More turmoil.

We panic when things go wrong.

We fight with our loved ones—kicking aside anything that remotely resembles love.

We medicate ourselves by acting on impulses, indulging our compulsions, and using drugs.

We grow weary, we grow dull, we grow even more stressed—and we blame God, even as we're blaming each other.

It doesn't have to be this way.

Healing Steps

Slow down. If you find your family running from event to event, it's time to slow down and rethink your priorities. Consider ways of decreasing the stress in your home by scheduling plenty of downtime.

Practice relaxation techniques together. Work with your child to figure out what helps her relax most. If she finds herself stressed or worried often, develop a "What to Do When I'm Feeling Worried" action plan she can use to stop the worry cycle.

Talk through what's bugging your child—especially issues or situations dealing with self-esteem, identity, and his relationships with friends. Be his advocate without embarrassing him.

Talk proactively with your child about how to deal with mistakes and failures as well as victories and team playing. Always take immediate action if the issue is bullying.[2]

Healing Words for Growth

Healing Words for My Family (and How I Plan to Use Them):

_____

_____

_____

_____

Healing Words for Growth:

_____

_____

_____

_____

Healing Words to Pray:

_____

_____

_____

_____

22

Resolving Conflict: The Ephesians 4:26 Principle

*In your anger do not sin: Do not let the
sun go down while you are still angry.*
EPHESIANS 4:26

Even though many Christians feel uncomfortable expressing anger, the Bible actually offers guidelines on getting angry the *right* way. It's up to you to teach your family what scripture says, beginning with Ephesians 4:26–27. In this passage Paul tells us, " 'In your anger, do not sin': Do not let the sun go down while you are still angry, and do not give the devil a foothold."

This passage makes it clear that anger isn't the sin. It's what that anger can *lead* to if your family doesn't head it off with God's help.

> → **What kinds of things spark quarrels in your home?
> How do you restore peace?**

Healing Journey

"Why do I get blamed for *everything*?" your son screams.

You cross your arms and lock eyes with him. "Watch your tone, young man," you say in a low, stern voice. "You're not *always* blamed, but you are the oldest in this family—and you know better. I want you to set a good example."

Suddenly you sense movement behind you. Your younger boy has taken cover behind you, and you don't have to turn around to know he's silently antagonizing his older brother again.

"Did you see that?" your older son gasps. "Maggot is doing it again."

"Oh, give it a rest," you respond. "Why can't you two get along? Why do you insist on turning our house into a battle zone?"

Your teen son gasps again. Just before slamming his bedroom door, he launches one last missile: "Not only is Maggot treated better, but you and Dad let him get away with murder."

Once inside his room, your teen son flops on his bed and buries his face in his pillow. He's convinced that you conceived his little brother just to spy on him.

"He's like a miniature Secret Service agent," your son grumbles to himself. "Just when I thought I could trust him, he tells Mom what I did last week—and I get grounded for the next three years. And as Mom pronounces punishment, that ever-so-faint smile plays across Maggot's lips. Oh, if I could just get my hands on those lips."

Your son flops on his bed and begins to throw a Nerf ball against his Colorado Rockies poster.

" 'No-o-o-o-o,' " he rumbles in his best prison warden voice. " 'You *can't* have that, you *can't* go there, you *can't* hang out with those friends!' When will they learn I'm *not* a little kid anymore?"

During supper he barely says two sentences—one of which is, "Pass the potatoes—please." Later, after his homework is completed, he doesn't watch TV with the family. Instead, he shuts his bedroom door and loses himself in his music collection.

Meanwhile, you collapse in the easy chair and squeeze your eyes shut. *Why do we go through this every time I say the word* no? you ask yourself as you replay the argument in your head. *Why do I always come off as the prison warden? Why can't we have a peaceful relationship?*[1]

• • •

Are you a parent who feels at the end of your rope too? We're not surprised if you're nodding your head yes, because similar parent-kid conflicts are played out countless times a day in households coast to coast. But to echo this parent's concern, "What's going on?"

Good question.

How is it possible for a houseful of people to love each other so much, yet at times feel as if they can't stand each other?

Why is it that we can live under the same roof with our spouses, sons, and daughters and can be so close to them—which means we know all of their strange quirks—yet sometimes feel like complete strangers?

The answer is obvious: An emotional war has erupted between many parents and their children, specifically between parents and teens. It's that "war of independence," a perfectly normal phase of growing up. With each step the boy or girl in your life takes on the path to adulthood, he or she becomes more and more independent of Mom and Dad.

But in the meantime, how can you survive the daily storms on your home front? And when it comes to the specific needs of teenagers, what can you do to cool down the hot spots and even improve your relationship with them? Following are a few ideas.

Healing Steps

Allow for a cooling-off period. Unless you detect some serious disrespect, a little bit of the "cold shoulder treatment" from your child won't hurt. True, it doesn't feel too good, but your child needs a chance to cool off and to process the situation. (For that matter, you need to cool off as well.) Give them time to cool off, but. . .

Don't let them shut down for too long. Too much of the cold shoulder treatment and you could end up with even more tension later on. After a fair amount of time has passed, make an effort to get your child talking about the disagreement. Communicating and listening will ultimately open the doors to greater understanding.

Let them know that they are on your "most wanted" list. Say something like this: "If you feel as though you're on our 'most wanted' list, you're right! Regardless of all the conflicts we'll experience together, you really are *wanted* by us. We really do love you."

Help them understand that it's okay to be angry sometimes. Point to Christ as an example. Explain to your son or daughter that several times during His ministry, Jesus became angry with the scribes and Pharisees. Why? Because they taught people to follow the wrong path to God and thus led those people straight to the gates of hell.

Teach them to be angry without sinning. While most kids know how to get angry, it's this second step they need to work on. Help your children express their anger the right way. In other words, the silent treatment and screaming matches don't accomplish anything. If something is important enough to get mad about, then it's important enough to try to work out the conflict.

Encourage your kids to. . .

- shift their focus away from the emotion and concentrate on dealing with the situation as Jesus would.
- channel the anger into constructive action. . .such as finding a workable solution instead of letting angry words or actions escalate into a bigger problem.

Healing Words for Growth

Healing Words for My Family (and How I Plan to Use Them):

_____

_____

_____

_____

Healing Words for Growth:

_____

_____

_____

_____

Healing Words to Pray:

_____

_____

_____

_____

23

Integrity: Marks of a Thriving Family

Whoever walks in integrity walks securely,
but whoever takes crooked paths will be found out.
PROVERBS 10:9

Integrity is central to the life of a Christian. And as parents, we must set the example in our homes. We must communicate to our families that being real through and through is one of the most important characteristics of God's people. As the body of Christ, we must model honesty and integrity to the world.

God sees every action and hears every word we speak—even those uttered from lying lips. Though we may be able to deceive others, we simply cannot lie to God—not now, not ever.

Let's examine the root of a lie and reveal its impact on your family.

→ **What is the opposite of integrity? Have you or a family member ever told a "little white lie" or justified an action that you know is wrong? Explain your answer. List the ways that lying or cheating can harm your family.**

Healing Journey

Jordan pours milk onto his cereal, digs his spoon into the bowl, and pauses. The teen is worried.

A geometry exam is hanging over his head, along with an appetite-robbing realization: students who don't memorize the fundamental theorems at the beginning of the semester have no hope of passing the midterm exam.

Jordan knows he's in trouble. *Time,* he tells himself, *gotta buy more time to study.*

"Dad, uh, I was wondering—"

"Hold up, sport," his father responds as he presses a cell phone to his ear. "Mr. Johnson? Bill here. Hey, listen, I'm on my way, but I'm stuck in traffic," he says with a wink at his son. Jordan rolls his eyes.

"Yeah, it's a mess out here," he adds, taking one last gulp of coffee. "I'm definitely going to be late, so do me a favor and hold down the fort, okay?"

Just as Jordan begins to speak again, his mom steps into kitchen waving a check in her hand.

"Hon, here's that deposit for the men's retreat next month," she tells her husband. "It was due two weeks ago, so I backdated it. We didn't have the money at the time, but we can make up some excuse. They'll see the date and let you in—I'm sure of it."

Jordan's mom glances at her son. "You look upset, sweetie. Is everything all right?"

Jordan swallows hard then clears his throat. "Well, see, I have this big test today, but I'm not ready. Can one of you please, please call the school and make up an excuse for me? Maybe you can say that Grandma is sick or tell them—"

"A lie?" Jordan's mom interrupts.

"Hold up, mister," his dad chimes in. "You know that's off-limits in this household."

Jordan's mouth drops open. "You're joking, right?"

"Absolutely not!" his mom says, slightly red-faced.

"Son, where did you get the idea that lying is okay?" his dad asks.

Jordan fidgets in his chair then looks down at a soggy mass that was once his breakfast. "Well, actually," he says, unsure of the right words to use, "to be totally honest, I kinda learned it from, well—

The teen looks up, his eyes bouncing between his mom and dad. "I sorta got the idea from. . .*you!*"

• • •

Everybody stretches the truth and tells little white lies from time to time, right? Presidents, network news anchormen, even famous religious leaders. And if occasional "exaggerations" deliver positive outcomes, how can they hurt?

Consider this: The Bible makes it clear that God hates a lying tongue.

- *"The LORD detests lying lips, but he delights in people who are trustworthy" (Proverbs 12:22).*
- *"Whoever of you loves life and desires to see many good days, keep your tongue from evil and your lips from telling lies" (Psalm 34:12–13).*

God wants integrity, not compromise. Nearly every day our families face choices that show others, and God, where honesty and integrity rate in our lives. The temptation to stretch the truth—or tell only half of it—is always staring us in the face. And at times, lying may seem like our only option, especially if we feel stressed or threatened in some way. And for some, lying has become a habit. We've gotten comfortable stretching the truth.

But it doesn't have to be this way. The Bible shares the key to pursuing integrity: "being confident of this, that he who began a good work in you will carry it on to completion until the day of Christ Jesus" (Philippians 1:6).

Healing Steps

Our heavenly Father is quick to offer forgiveness when we ask for it. He understands our humanity, which is why He looks favorably upon those who strive to be honest.

A family that makes honesty a priority. . .

- *knows how to identify hypocrisy—and steer clear of it.* Phony faith is not hard to miss: we say one thing then act another way; we find faults in others but overlook our own; we call ourselves Christian but catch ourselves acting like the world.
- *seeks honesty at the deepest levels.* It's easy to bend the truth from time to time, stretching the facts to make something sound better. Yet as we strive to be honest, we must avoid those "tiny exaggerations" that so easily fly out of our mouths. After all, God cares about every detail of our lives—the big issues and the small.
- *desires integrity.* Be comforted, not fearful, by the fact that the Lord keeps us in His sight. He will guide our steps and guard our lips if we let Him. What does integrity look like? Share this

checklist with your family:

- Integrity serves as a guide in life's moral decisions (Proverbs 11:3).
- Integrity hates falsehood in every form (Proverbs 13:5–6).
- Integrity is something to be held on to, even in tough times (Job 2:3).
- Integrity keeps its word even when to do so hurts (Psalm 15:1–4).
- Integrity backs up what it says with how it lives (Titus 2:7).
- Integrity understands that all of life is on display before God (1 Kings 9:4).

Healing Words for Growth

Healing Words for My Family (and How I Plan to Use Them):

_____

_____

_____

_____

Healing Words for Growth:

_____

_____

_____

_____

Healing Words to Pray:

_____

_____

_____

_____

24

What to Say When Families Fracture

"At the beginning of creation God 'made them male and female.'
'For this reason a man will leave his father and mother and be united to
his wife, and the two will become one flesh.' So they are no longer two,
but one flesh. Therefore what God has joined together,
let no one separate."
MARK 10:6–9

If holy matrimony is a sacred, lifetime promise that men and women make before God, why is it so casually broken in today's world? And why are more and more husbands and wives viewing the marriage covenant as a legal contract—one that can be amended (or ended) at a later date?

Too often "as long as we both shall live" is replaced with "as long as we both shall love." The couple agrees to share all thing mutually until one or the other no longer wants to continue in the relationship. At that time they simply file the proper documents in court and are released from the contract. Property, friends, and children are divided up between the two former lovers—and everybody lives happily ever after, right?

Wrong!

Viewing marriage as a mere contractual agreement results in misery for everyone involved, especially for family and friends. Victims of broken homes feel overwhelming stress, including a deep sense of abandonment— scars they end up carrying into adulthood. Each divorce is like the death of a small civilization.

→ Can you see how the breakup of the family unit can eventually destroy a nation? Describe how divorce has impacted you. (Perhaps directly. . .or through a friend or relative.) What healing words do you communicate when a family fractures?

Healing Journey

As a child, I (Michael) was the victim of a fractured family. And the scars that I bear to this day connect to the immobilizing emotions of fear and worry.

My father abandoned my family when I was just six years old. And in the years that followed, I watched my mom worry her way through what must have felt like an impossible job: she had to raise six kids all by herself! I was the youngest and certainly the most high maintenance of her children.

"Mrs. Ross, that boy of yours is such a worrywart," my first-grade teacher once told her during parent-teacher conferences. Then she grabbed my mom's hand. "Is everything okay at home? How are you holding up?" I held my breath—selfishly worried that Mom would say something that would make us—actually *me*—seem different, inferior. *Will my teacher stop liking us? Will the other kids think we're weird?* (As an adult, I've cut myself some slack. After all, first graders aren't supposed to worry; they're supposed to have a childhood. Sadly, I didn't.)

Junior high was a nightmare. "Come on, Ross—don't be so scared of the ball," barked Mr. Battle, my PE instructor. (Yep—his name was actually *Battle*, which ironically described the hell I endured day after day.) "Man up. Put some muscle into it." During moments like that, I would have given anything to melt into the cracks on the gym floor. *Sorry, Mr. Battle, but I don't exactly feel much like a man. Most of the time, I just feel scared.*

College was better. "This boy can write," one of my professors told me—in front of a classroom filled with my peers. And then he proceeded to read something I had written. It was my first journalism assignment, and my professor was a hard-nosed newsman who seemed otherwise impossible to please. The affirmation built me up—until negative self-talk and a debilitating cycle of fear brought me down again. *But what kind of a future will I have? The competition is fierce among writers. And don't most of them starve?*

My own marriage changed everything. "You know it's all going to be okay," my wife, Tiffany, often tells me. "God is in control. Do you actually believe this? All the worry in the world isn't going to change a thing. It won't bring us more money or make us more acceptable. . .or cure a terminal illness. Can you take a faith step and trust Him with the things that worry you? Can you trust Him enough to release all these fear traps?" Praise God for godly women! Praise God for life-mates we can lean on, lovers who gently nudge us back to the cross. Tiffany really knows me—the person I am inside—worry warts and all—yet she loves me anyway. I don't have to perform or mask my flaws. I am acceptable just as I am.

• • •

As a child, I was the victim of a fractured family. But as an adult, I am healing.

The types of emotions that God is mending in my life relate to apprehension, fear, worry, and anxiety. They can range in severity from mere twinges of uneasiness to full-blown panic attacks marked by rapid heartbeat, trembling, sweating, queasiness, and terror. Sometimes these feelings are connected to everyday worries and strike out of the blue ("free-floating anxiety"). Sometimes they are a bit more out of proportion, even unrealistic, and are triggered by specific struggles ("situational anxiety"). For example, the abandonment I experienced as a child makes me especially sensitive to issues of death and loss.

"People who suffer from anxiety are especially prone to engage in fearful self-talk," explains Edmund Bourne, PhD, who specializes in the treatment of anxiety disorders. "Anxiety can be generated on the spur of the moment by repeatedly making statements to yourself that begin with the two words: 'what if.' "[1]

Yet God is teaching me to surrender fear and worry—and He is replacing them with faith. Some healing words from loved ones have helped me along the way: consider communicating these messages and practical steps to those you know whose families have fractured.

Healing Steps

Be empathetic. My wife nudges me closer to God, and God nudges me deeper into His wisdom: "Trust in the LORD with all your heart and lean not on your own understanding" (Proverbs 3:5). And his wisdom is transformational.

Use positive self-talk. When I begin to feel immobilized by catastrophic thoughts—*What if nobody likes me? What if I fail? What if I lose the ones I love?*—I neutralize fear with positive self-talk. For example, I might tell myself something like this:

"*Live*, don't live in fear."

"Relax—and trust God."

"Believe in God's truth, not the lies you are thinking."

"Know that God is in control."

"Be still and know that *he* is God" (see Psalm 46:10).

Prayer. I usually have conversations with Jesus all throughout the day—as I drive, as I write, before I head into meetings, during prayer and Bible studies. I especially pray when fear, worry, and anxiety invade my thoughts. For me, this is the single most effective step. And when anxiety flairs up, my prayer may go something like this: "Dear Jesus, I need Your strength, protection, and truth right now. You know what I'm feeling. Keep Satan away from me. Heal my heart; heal my mind. In Jesus name, I pray. Amen."

God's Word. I use "spiritual interruptions" throughout the day to combat my struggles. As scripture is worked into my life, God begins speaking to me intimately—guiding me, changing me. The Bible has a supernatural component that no one can explain. It has to be experienced (see 2 Timothy 3:14–17; Hebrews 4:12–13).

Empowerment. Through the power of the Holy Spirit I am protected from the enemy's attacks. I don't have to roll over and play dead. I can overcome anxiety, worry, fear, and any other soul-robbing choice. The truth is, we all have a choice. We are responsible for how we feel and behave (barring physiological factors). It's what we say to ourselves in response to any particular situation that mainly determines our mood and feelings.[2]

Healing Words for Growth

Healing Words for My Family (and How I Plan to Use Them):

_____

_____

_____

_____

Healing Words for Growth:

_____

_____

_____

_____

Healing Words to Pray:

_____

_____

_____

_____

25

Father Hunger: Healing Messages Kids Need

Children, obey your parents in the Lord, for this is right. "Honor your
father and mother"—which is the first commandment with a promise—
"so that it may go well with you and that you may enjoy long life
on the earth." Fathers, do not exasperate your children; instead,
bring them up in the training and instruction of the Lord.
EPHESIANS 6:1–4

Most of us think we know what good fathering looks like. Usually images of fictional dads come to mind: Ty Burrell's playful Phil Dunphy in *Modern Family*; Jimmy Stewart (George Bailey in *It's a Wonderful Life*); Hugh Beaumont (Ward Cleaver in *Leave It to Beaver*).

But get this: there's no substitute for the real thing. Even though our kids often idolize athletes, musicians, and actors, what they really want—and need—is a dad who loves them.

An available, loving father guides, nurtures, and strengthens his children in three key ways:

- He offers a positive model of manhood.
- He builds his child's self-concept.
- He shapes a child's faith and values.

Spending time with our children is the best thing a man can do for his family. And you don't have to do anything elaborate. Simple daily connections can have a profound and lasting impact. Shoot hoops together, take walks, grab a soda—anything! But make sure you give your child ample opportunity to talk. And remember this: your kids want and need your attention but often just don't know how to ask for it.

As I (Brian) minister to adult men through the men's equipping ministry Iron Sharpens Iron, I have discovered that more than 50 percent of

American men have had marginal to poor (or even worse) relationships with their biological fathers. They were constantly told—and still remember—reckless words from their dads. Most can't recall words of blessing and encouragement. These adult men are then called to bless and encourage their own kids, yet they don't know where to begin. What's more, they still carry wounds that need to heal. Here's the good news: these kinds of memories can be healed as men get connected to their heavenly Father. Jesus accepts them and loves them just as they are. He even provides a way for them to experience forgiveness and healing. These are the kinds of messages I strive to communicate to the men in my care. And they are the kinds of healing words I encourage them to speak into their own families.

→ **What should you do if an emotional "invisible wall" has gone up between you and your child? How can you rekindle your connection? What are some healing words your family needs to hear from you?**

Healing Journey

Scene 1: A Star in the Making

A smoke-filled stage in Kansas City explodes with pyrotechnics and computerized laser lights. A teen drama troupe decked out in flashy costumes jumps, rolls, tumbles, and dances onto the scene. Their high-action performance bursts with a frenzied mix of dramatic elements: ballet, music, and mime.

Backstage, the adrenaline is running just as high in the star performer. Sixteen-year-old Terry, who plays the lead role, limbers up her legs prior to making her entrance. The second she gets her cue, Terry steps under a spotlight and launches into character. She's met with thundering applause.

Right on the front row, one of the young woman's biggest fans—her proud father—is clapping and cheering the loudest.

"Break a leg!" Terry's dad shouts with a wink. He bows his head and whispers a prayer: "Lord, please give my daughter the courage and confidence to do well. And let her perform for your glory, not hers. Above all, let Terry know how valued she is to You—and to us. Amen."

Scene 2: Campfire Conversations

There's nothing quite like a campfire to get guys talking. Staring into glowing embers beneath an infinite canopy of stars has a way of moving a man's soul beyond the mundane and onto the ultimate issues of life. That's how it was for Jeffery and Jonathan—a father and son who spent the day with several other families rafting a twisting, churning Colorado river. Now safe at camp, they relive their adventure.

"I'm so proud of you, Jonathan, for trusting me today," Jeffery told his son. "We were a solid team, which is how God wants us to be."

Jonathan smiled and put his arm around his father. "My heart was racing, and I felt so scared when I saw the rapids," he said. "But you stayed calm. That really helped. And when we came through okay, it gave me more confidence."

The teen paused and thought carefully about his words and then continued. "I wish it could be this way at home. It's like, there's so much stress. Your job, Mom saying we have more bills than money, pressure at school, the way we fight sometimes. Maybe we can start handling troubles like we did today."

Another father, Paul, vowed to spend more time with his seventeen-year-old son, David. "We get busy with each of us moving fast and in so many different directions," he says. "We've got to slow down and stay connected. We've got to do a better job of being a family."

David then opened up for the first time about his biggest fears. "The other kids are brutal," he said. "The constant teasing and bullying, the stupid cliques, the struggle to fit in—I get so sick of it all. I just want to live a normal life."

"I didn't realize that life has been so tough for you," responded Paul, "but we're going to work through these troubles—together."

• • •

Whether your child steals the show on stage or braves the rapids in the wilderness, a father must communicate an essential truth about his child's identity: The boy or girl in your life is a high-value kid.

Like wet clay, your child is still malleable, explains pastor and author

Paul W. Swets. And as they move through childhood and into the teen years, they enter "a new and qualitatively different realm of thinking, feeling, and acting. It is confusing but exciting."[1] And they need their fathers' knowledge and support to survive.

The key to launching your children successfully into adulthood depends on the applause they receive from Dad. Are you instilling confidence in the lives of your children? Are you affirming the unique individuals God has created them to be?

Applaud your "star in the making."

Healing Steps

Tune into their feelings. Try to look at events at home or at school from your child's point of view. If your son or daughter senses that you don't really understand or care, they will stop listening to you. But when it's clear that you're doing your best to understand, the chances are much greater that they will tune in to you. Despite how it feels at times, children—even teenagers—really do want their parents to talk to them; they want to believe they have someone who will listen, who will understand, who will make them feel better.

Give them your blessing. Jesus was in a river when He received this blessing: "This is my Son, whom I love; with him I am well pleased" (Matthew 3:17). If the Son of God received a verbal stamp of approval from His Father, then we can all benefit from affirmation. "I'm proud of you. I love you. I enjoy watching God shape you into the amazing person you are." There's special power when those words come from the mouths of fathers, and even the most cantankerous kids admit they long to hear approval from their moms and dads.

The blessings of a parent will impact a young person all the days of his or her life. God has created parents to carry more influence than any other human being, and a righteous parent must step in and embrace that role. Proverbs 10:21 says, "The lips of the righteous nourish many." To nourish means to cherish, to cultivate, to nurture. This is the role of a parent and of mentors in a child's life.

Be willing to say you're sorry. Face it: no parent is perfect. When fathers blow it with their kids—breaking promises or flying off the handle—they should be willing to admit it and ask for forgiveness. Humility and openness are the foundation for a healthy relationship between a parent and child.

Build positive memories. Being careful not to say the wrong words to your children is not enough. Each parent must take on the challenge to create positive memories by nourishing their children with words both verbally and in writing. This is especially important for children as they make their transitions so they know without a doubt the unconditional love of their parents.

Pray daily for your child. Fathers should not only pray *for* their kids, but pray *with* them, as well. While this sounds like a no-brainer, it's amazing how many families neglect this important activity.

Healing Words for Growth

Healing Words for My Family (and How I Plan to Use Them):

_____

_____

_____

_____

Healing Words for Growth:

_____

_____

_____

_____

Healing Words to Pray:

_____

_____

_____

_____

26

Becoming the Proverbs 31 Mother

Charm is deceptive, and beauty is fleeting; but a woman who fears the LORD is to be praised. Honor her for all that her hands have done, and let her works bring her praise at the city gate.
PROVERBS 31:30–31

When I (Michael) think of my mother—and the profound influence she has on so many people—Proverbs 31 comes to mind. While this passage talks about "a wife of noble character," the verses highlight some qualities and spiritual principles that all women can apply. But keep in mind, these verses refer to the ideal. They are great goals for which to strive, but it's unreal to think you can fulfill all of them at the same time. (Hey, God doesn't expect you to be a superwoman!)

The Proverbs 31 woman. . .

Is trustworthy (verse 10): reliable, consistent, secure, realistic.

Is virtuous (verse 11): morally upright, learns from past mistakes and keeps her principles.

Is industrious (verses 13, 14, 28): hardworking, diligent, active, persistent. She hangs in there with tough tasks when her body and mind tell her to quit.

Is generous (verse 15): unselfish, considerate, kindhearted, ungrudging, always willing to give or share.

Is wise (verse 16, 27): perceptive, intuitive, thoughtful, shrewd, aims for practical, God-honoring goals.

Is strong (verse 17): Stable, sure of herself, has the ability to juggle many different tasks under pressure.

Is compassionate (verse 20): sympathetic, responsive, warm. She is willing to offer constructive help.

Is dignified (verse 28): stands tall with grace, poised.

Is spiritual (verse 30): fears God and reverences her relationship with Him above everything else.

→ **Which of these attributes are hard for you to live out?
Which ones come natural for you? Describe a woman
in your life who possesses many of these qualities.**

Healing Journey

It was Christmas Eve—a joyful time, a family time. So why did I feel so depressed? For one thing, my mom and I were alone.

I was seventeen, and my five older siblings (three brothers and two sisters) were grown up and out of the house—and unable to come home for the holidays. As for my father, he had deserted my family when I was a young boy.

The truth is, Dad was an alcoholic—and Mom would never allow alcohol in our house. So, at about the time I was learning to ride a bike, Mom was forced to take a tough love approach: "Get help, and learn to be a proper husband and father," she told my dad, "or follow your addiction—and lose your family. You can't have both."

My father chose his addiction. It was a decision that broke our hearts and cracked the foundation of my family. Yet in the years that followed, my mother was determined to mend some of the fractures and to hold our family together. I'm happy to say, she succeeded. (To this day, my brothers, sisters, and I share a deep bond that was nurtured by our mother.)

But on this particular Christmas, I didn't feel very festive. I missed the chaotic "Grand Central Station" atmosphere that usually filled our house.

"Yep, this is going to be a sorry holiday," I mumbled to myself as I slouched in a recliner and stared glumly at our Christmas tree.

Does this thing actually have branches? I wondered. Our tree was covered with so many ornaments and candy canes and strands of popcorn, it was nearly impossible to see anything that was remotely spruce-like.

I squinted, noticing a brightly colored decoration that I had made years earlier—then a few that were created by my sisters. *Mom has saved them all,* I thought to myself. *This tree is like a timeline of our lives.*

As I followed the "timeline," memories began to flood my mind. Mostly good ones.

My eyes focused on an oddly shaped antique bulb that was passed down from my grandmother. I couldn't help thinking about all the family traditions my mom had established. She was so proud of our heritage. (My relatives could be traced back to England, Scotland, and Sweden.)

I spotted a furry, hand-stitched reindeer my mom had made—which triggered images of the long hours she worked cooking, cleaning, and doing everything possible to keep a roof over our heads.

Suddenly my thoughts were interrupted by the sweet smell of chocolate—then a warm smile.

"Let's open a gift," my mom said, handing me a cup of cocoa. "We always open one present on Christmas Eve—and this year shouldn't be any different." Before I had a chance to utter a word, she plopped a big package on my lap.

"No, Mom, let's just forget about it," I protested. "Everything's all wrong this year."

Mom lifted an eyebrow. "I'd say things are pretty right," she pointed out.

I shook my head and groaned. My mom continued talking.

"Look around you," she said. "Look at where you live, and consider the food you get to eat. Some people in the world don't have any of these things. And think about the people who love you—like your brothers and sisters. They may not be here physically, but we're still a family. A strong family."

Secretly I was tracking with everything my mom had to say, but my teenage pride wouldn't allow me to admit it. Instead, I glanced at the package on my lap and gently began tugging at the ribbon. When the last piece of wrapping paper fell to the floor, the gift was revealed.

I looked up and gasped. "Mom—you can't afford this!"

"I'm the gift giver here, so I'll decide what I can and can't afford."

My mom had practically emptied her savings account on a present I had talked endlessly about for years yet had always thought was out of reach. She bought me a 35mm camera, along with various lenses.

"Every young journalist should learn to use a camera, right?" Mom asked.

I sat speechless, feeling as if I was holding more than just a camera—but some sort of link to my future. "This is amazing!" I said as I fiddled with the lenses.

"There's a carrying bag in the box, too," Mom said. "I figure you can take this to college with you next year."

A grin stretched across my face. "Mom, *you're* pretty amazing. You sacrifice so much for us. What would we do without you? Who would we be?"

Suddenly Christmas didn't seem so empty. I began to see my mom differently. For the first time during my teen years, I began to respect the incredible woman God created her to be. And from that moment on, my world began to make a lot more sense.

• • •

That night I unwrapped the greatest gift a teen could ever receive. Of course I don't mean an expensive camera. I'm talking about the gift only a nurturing woman like my mother can give: hope.

Despite the hardships in our lives, my mom did everything possible to shape her children into men and women who were ready to face the world with confidence. She planted seeds of faith in our lives and sparked in us a vision for the future.

Healing Steps

Strive to be a "woman of noble character." With God's help, you can become the woman God desires you to be. Use Proverbs 31 as a standard to reach for, knowing that you don't have to fulfill every detail in every verse.

Put God above everything in life. Regardless of your gifts and goals, make sure Proverbs 30:30 is true for you: "A woman who fears the LORD is to be praised."

Healing Words for Growth

Healing Words for My Family (and How I Plan to Use Them):

_____

_____

_____

_____

Healing Words for Growth:

_____

_____

_____

_____

Healing Words to Pray:

_____

_____

_____

_____

27

Essential Words for Wives

*Identifying my many roles isn't always easy: I'm a wife, a mother,
a songwriter, and a storyteller. And some describe me as a preacher
whose pulpit is a piano bench. Each of these titles describes me. . . .
As a CCM artist, I feel that I'm part of something much bigger than
myself. It's God's math. The Lord multiplies everything so people I've
never met before in places I've never traveled to are being affected.
Not that if I quit the ministry, the world would fall apart.
But I do know if I don't play my part, people miss out.*

SARA GROVES[1]

GENEROUS

Proverbs 31:20–21: "She opens her arms to the poor and extends her hands
to the needy. When it snows, she has no fear for her household; for all of
them are clothed in scarlet."

Family: Express that you notice the generosity and sacrifices of the
wife and mother in your life.

Wives: Reflect on this scripture and ask God to help you live these
qualities.

KIND

Ephesians 4:32: "Be kind and compassionate to one another, forgiving each
other, just as in Christ God forgave you."

Family: Express how much you've grown because of the generosity
and kindness of the wife and mother in your life.

Wives: Reflect on this scripture and ask God to help you forgive
others.

NOBLE

Proverbs 31:10–12: "A wife of noble character who can find? She is worth far more than rubies. Her husband has full confidence in her and lacks nothing of value. She brings him good, not harm, all the days of her life."

Family: Express how much you love and value the wife and mother in your life.

Wives: Reflect on this scripture and ask God to help you be a wife of noble character.

REVERENT

Titus 2:3–5: "Likewise, teach the older women to be reverent in the way they live, not to be slanderers or addicted to much wine, but to teach what is good. Then they can urge the younger women to love their husbands and children, to be self-controlled and pure, to be busy at home, to be kind, and to be subject to their husbands, so that no one will malign the word of God."

Family: Express how proud and appreciative you are of the wife and mother in your life.

Wives: Reflect on this scripture and ask God to help you practice these virtues and teach them to others.

TRUSTWORTHY

1 Timothy 3:11: "In the same way, the women are to be worthy of respect, not malicious talkers but temperate and trustworthy in everything."

Family: Express how much you respect and trust the wife and mother in your life.

Wives: Reflect on this scripture and ask God to help you behave as one worthy of respect.

WISE

Proverbs 31:26: "She speaks with wisdom, and faithful instruction is on her tongue."

Family: Express how much you enjoy the wisdom and faithfulness of the wife and mother in your life.

Wives: Reflect on this scripture and ask God to help you grow in wisdom.

Wives, Plant These Words and Grow

Nourish spiritual growth with God's Word. Here's what Hebrews 12:1 instructs us to do: "Let us throw off everything that hinders. . . . And let us run with perseverance the race marked out for us." Face it, growing spiritually and becoming more like Christ isn't easy, is it? It's a bit like running an ultra-marathon that's filled with giant potholes and steep, winding trails. And like Sara Groves, you wear many hats, stepping in and out of a variety of different roles—all in a single day! But as a Christ-follower, you're "part of something much bigger." In the days ahead, do the following:

Plot a course for growth. List your goals:
In one month I want to. . .
In six months I want to. . .
In one year I want to. . .

List ten steps that you will take to grow (and reach your goals above):
1. _____
2. _____
3. _____
4. _____
5. _____
6. _____
7. _____
8. _____
9. _____
10. _____

28

Essential Words for Husbands

This mission of introducing one's children to the Christian faith can be likened to a three-man relay race. . . . My most important reason for living is to get the baton—the gospel—safely in the hands of my children. Of course, I want to place it in as many other hands as possible, and I'm deeply devoted to the ministry to families that God has given me. Nevertheless, my number one responsibility is to evangelize my own children. In the words of my dad, everything else appears "pale and washed out" when compared with that fervent desire. Unless my son and daughter grasp the faith and take it with them around the track, it matters little how fast they run. Being first across the finish line is meaningless unless they carry the baton with them.

—DR. JAMES DOBSON[1]

DEVOTED

John 15:9–13: "As the Father has loved me, so have I loved you. Now remain in my love. If you keep my commands, you will remain in my love, just as I have kept my Father's commands and remain in his love. I have told you this so that my joy may be in you and that your joy may be complete. My command is this: Love each other as I have loved you. Greater love has no one than this: to lay down one's life for one's friends."

> **Family:** Express how thankful you are for the devotion and sharing spirit that are modeled by the husband and father in your life.
>
> **Husbands:** Reflect on this scripture and ask God to help you lay down your life daily for your wife and family.

HUMBLE

Philippians 2:5–8: "Have the same mindset as Christ Jesus: Who, being in very nature God, did not consider equality with God something to be used to his own advantage; rather, he made himself nothing by taking the very nature of a servant, being made in human likeness. And being found in appearance as a man, he humbled himself by becoming obedient to death— even death on a cross!"

> **Family:** Express how much you appreciate the humility and serving spirit of the husband and father in your life.
>
> **Husbands:** Reflect on this scripture and ask God to help you follow Christ's example as you care for your family.

LOVING

Ephesians 5:25: "Husbands, love your wives, just as Christ loved the church and gave himself up for her."

> **Family:** Express your appreciation for the love and sacrifices of the husband and father in your life.
>
> **Husbands:** Reflect on this scripture and ask God to help you love your family as Christ loves you.

PROTECTOR

Isaiah 25:4: "You have been a refuge for the poor, a refuge for the needy in their distress, a shelter from the storm and a shade from the heat."

> **Family:** Express how much safer you feel because of the protection and emotional strength you receive from the husband and father in your life.
>
> **Husbands:** Reflect on this scripture and ask God to help you to be a shelter from the storms for those in your care.

SELFLESS

Ecclesiastes 4:9–11: "Two are better than one, because they have a good return for their labor: If either of them falls down, one can help the other up. But pity anyone who falls and has no one to help them up. Also, if two lie down together, they will keep warm. But how can one keep warm alone?"

> **Family:** Express how supported you feel because of the selflessness and care of the husband and father in your life.

Husbands: Reflect on this scripture and ask God to help you share a deeper connection with your wife and children.

SERVANT LEADER

Ephesians 5:23: "For the husband is the head of the wife as Christ is the head of the church, his body, of which he is the Savior."

Family: Express how much you value the support and provision of the husband and father in your life.

Husbands: Reflect on this scripture and ask God to give you discernment as you guide and provide for your family.

Husbands, Plant These Words and Grow

Nourish spiritual growth with God's Word. Proverbs 20:7 says this about the eternal influence of a godly husband and father: "The righteous lead blameless lives; blessed are their children after them." And a few chapters later, Proverbs 22:6 gives parents their most important assignment: "Start children off on the way they should go, and even when they are old they will not turn from it." A godly father delights in, loves, corrects, instructs, disciplines, provides for, leads, and contributes a legacy to his children.[2] According to Dr. James Dobson, our number one responsibility is to evangelize our own children. Love your wife and invest in your kids. Give them your time, your encouragement—and your legacy of faith.

In the days ahead, do the following:

Plot a course for growth. List your goals:
In one month I want to. . .
In six months I want to. . .
In one year I want to. . .

List ten steps that you will take to grow (and reach your goals above):

1. _____

2. _____

3. _____

4. _____

5. _____

6. _____

7. _____

8. _____

9. _____

10. _____

29

Essential Words for Children

Children are likely to live up to what you believe of them.
LADY BIRD JOHNSON[1]

BLESSING

Psalm 127:3–5 (ESV): "Behold, children are a heritage from the LORD, the fruit of the womb, a reward. Like arrows in the hand of a warrior are the children of one's youth. Blessed is the man who fills his quiver with them! He shall not be put to shame when he speaks with his enemies in the gate."

As a Family: Express how thankful you are for each member of your family.

Note to Parents: Encourage your child to think about how loved he or she is by you and by God.

GREATEST

Matthew 18:1–5: "At that time the disciples came to Jesus and asked, 'Who, then, is the greatest in the kingdom of heaven?' He called a little child to him, and placed the child among them. And he said: 'Truly I tell you, unless you change and become like little children, you will never enter the kingdom of heaven. Therefore, whoever takes the lowly position of this child is the greatest in the kingdom of heaven. And whoever welcomes one such child in my name welcomes me.' "

As a Family: Using this passage as a conversation starter, share reasons" why you think Jesus views children as the *greatest*.

Note to Parents: Encourage your child to think about the amazing act of love that Jesus showed us all when He went to the cross.

HEIR TO THE KINGDOM

Luke 18:16: "But Jesus called the children to him and said, 'Let the little children come to me, and do not hinder them, for the kingdom of God belongs to such as these.' "

> **As a Family:** Talk about a description of Christians that your children may not realize: Those who give their hearts to Jesus become a part of His royal family—they become heirs to the kingdom of God.

> **Note to Parents:** Encourage your kids to think about what it means to live daily as an heir to God's kingdom. (Hint: We follow Christ's example by obeying God, honoring Him, and striving to love others the way Jesus loves us.)

PEACEMAKER

Matthew 5:9: "Blessed are the peacemakers, for they will be called children of God."

> **As a Family:** Express how proud you are that each member of your family desires to live in peace with each other and with God.

> **Note to Parents:** Encourage your children to think about the difference between peace and turmoil—and especially which one God gives us.

TRUSTING

Matthew 11:25: "At that time Jesus said, 'I praise you, Father, Lord of heaven and earth, because you have hidden these things from the wise and learned, and revealed them to little children.' "

> **As a Family:** Express how wonderful it is that God sees and honors the faith of every member of your family.

> **Note to Parents:** Encourage your children to think about how important it is for us all to trust God.

WONDERFULLY MADE

Psalm 139:13–16 (ESV): "For you formed my inward parts; you knitted me together in my mother's womb. I praise you, for I am fearfully and wonderfully made. Wonderful are your works; my soul knows it very well. My frame was not hidden from you, when I was being made in secret, intricately woven in the depths of the earth. Your eyes saw my unformed substance; in your book were written, every one of them, the days that were formed for me, when as yet there was none of them."

As a Family: Express how important all human life is to God, and in particular, the children in your family.

Note to Parents: Encourage your children to think about how valuable he or she is to God.

Parents, Plant These Words in a Child's Heart

Nourish spiritual growth with God's Word. Deuteronomy 11:18–19 says, "Fix these words of mine in your hearts and minds; tie them as symbols on your hands and bind them on your foreheads. Teach them to your children, talking about them when you sit at home and when you walk along the road, when you lie down and when you get up." Teach them God's Word—truths such as, "But the fruit of the Spirit is love, joy, peace, forbearance, kindness, goodness, faithfulness, gentleness and self-control. Against such things there is no law" (Galatians 5:22–23). And as Lady Bird Johnson implied, your children are likely to live up to "what you believe of them."

In the days ahead, do the following:

Plot a course for growth with your child. List some goals:
In one month I want to. . .
In six months I want to. . .
In one year I want to. . .

List ten steps that your child can take to grow (and reach the goals above):

1. _____
2. _____
3. _____

4. _____

5. _____

6. _____

7. _____

8. _____

9. _____

10. _____

30

Ready to Rethink Our Connections with Family and Start Giving More to the Ones We Love?

If the Lord's table is the prototype of the family table, then, if I think in terms of the family table, I know that I cannot sit down to bread and wine until I've said I'm sorry, until reparations have been made, relations restored. When one of our children had done something particularly unworthy, if it had come out into the open before dinner, it there had been an "I'm sorry," and there had been acceptance, and love, then would follow the happiest dinner possible, full of laughter and fun. If there was something still hidden; if one child, or as sometimes happens, one parent, was out of joint with the family and the world, that would destroy the atmosphere of the whole meal.[1]

MADELEINE L'ENGLE

Chart a Healing Path toward Change

1. *Receive God's Word:* Read or listen to Isaiah 58.

2. *Reflect on Isaiah 58:6–9:* Pull these verses apart sentence by sentence, looking for God's personal message to you. Invite the Holy Spirit to speak to you.

> *"Is not this the kind of fasting I have chosen: to loose the chains of injustice and untie the cords of the yoke, to set the oppressed free and break every yoke? Is it not to share your food with the hungry and to provide the poor wanderer with shelter—when you see the naked, to clothe him, and not to turn away from your own flesh and blood? Then your light will break forth like the dawn, and your healing will quickly appear; then your righteousness will go before you, and the glory of the LORD will be your rear guard. Then you will call, and the LORD will answer; you will cry for help, and he will say: Here am I."*

3. *Engage in a conversation with God.* After a moment of silence before the Lord, write out a dialogue between you and Him. Begin with general thoughts and impressions.

Heavenly Father, here's how I feel about these verses:

_____

_____

Here's what's hard for me, God—what I don't understand:

_____

_____

Now relate these verses to your specific struggles within your home.

Here's what Isaiah 58 is telling me about Your power, Your mercy, Your desire to "loose the chains" in my family's life:

_____

_____

With Your help, Lord—and despite how hard it may be—here's how I will try to trust You today, to take a new step in a new direction with my spouse and my kids:

_____

_____

4. *Memorize Isaiah 58:11.* Repeat this verse to yourself as often as needed. Write it on an index card and post it within sight.

The LORD will guide you always; he will satisfy your needs in a sun-scorched land and will strengthen your frame. You will be like a well-watered garden, like a spring whose waters never fail.

5. *Respond to God's nudges.* Try this exercise to promote deeper connections and trust within your family.

- *Be self-aware and painfully honest*—especially about who we are and what attracts us. Transparency, transparency, transparency is crucial during this step if we hope to change. Our tendency is to save face, justify and excuse our behavior, and reveal only part of the problem. Don't make that mistake. We'd be wise to take off our masks, bear all before God, and let Him get to the root of the issue. Begin with some questions.

- *Remember what God really thinks of us.* As sinners, we are all "foreigners" and "children of wrath." Yet, according to Ephesians 2, the Lord forgave our rebellion against Him. And Romans 5:8 says that even while we were still rejecting God, Jesus died for us. Christ looked down at those who nailed Him to a cross and cried out, "Father, forgive them, for they do not know what they are doing" (Luke 23:34). God wants to forgive our sins so we can spend eternity with Him. (Check out Exodus 34:6–7.)

- *Remember that God is our true Father—our heavenly Father.* He loves us, cares for us, equips us, and stands with us in our trials. Understanding who we really are as His children will help give us the courage to be who He created us to be and to overcome the enemy who seeks to steal, kill, and destroy.

- *Feed on the Word of God and the truth found in the scriptures.* Memorizing scripture and even praying through scripture is powerful—especially when we are weak, tempted, and can't find a way of escape. Speak the name of Jesus when you pray, believing the scriptures that you are engaging, and standing on the promises given to you as a daughter or son of God.

- *Clue into our weaknesses and limits as a family.* This knowledge usually comes to us through experience and failure, and it's important that we learn from our failures and shortcomings. What are the hot-button issues within our family? How can we improve communication and build deeper connections with each other? Note: The Holy Spirit will guide us. He will reveal our "hot buttons" as He cleanses us, tears down old ways of thinking and renovates our "spiritual house."

Part Four

HEALING WORDS
FOR THE COMMUNITY

31

Go Ahead—Take an "Eternal Risk"

Therefore, since we are surrounded by such a great cloud of witnesses, let us throw off everything that hinders and the sin that so easily entangles. And let us run with perseverance the race marked out for us, fixing our eyes on Jesus, the pioneer and perfecter of faith. For the joy set before him he endured the cross, scorning its shame, and sat down at the right hand of the throne of God. Consider him who endured such opposition from sinners, so that you will not grow weary and lose heart.
HEBREWS 12:1–3

Have you taken an eternal risk for God? The thrill is there. The adrenaline flows. Your heart will race. But you'll also hear the God of the universe cheering you on—and that's the biggest thrill of all.

So what's an eternal risk? Author Max Lucado offers some clues: "One source of man's weariness is the pursuit of things that can never satisfy; but which one of us has not been caught up in that pursuit at some time in our life? Our passions, possessions and pride—these are all *dead* things. When we try to get life out of dead things, the result is only weariness and dissatisfaction."[1]

→ **What kinds of pursuits do you find most satisfying?
What is the race marked out for us (see Hebrews 12:1–3 above)?**

Healing Journey

"Rough water ahead—hold on!" shouts the jungle guide.

I (Michael) grip the side of the canoe as it tears through a mound of twisted branches clogging the narrow river. The boat begins to rock violently, and a few of the teens on board scream. I grin.

I'm not on a water ride at Disneyland. I'm actually three thousand miles from home, deep in the heart of Panama's Darien jungle—having the adventure of a lifetime. I'm here with a youth group on a two-week summer mission trip.

The canoe steadies itself and continues the five-hour trip up the Rio Chucunaque. I'm overwhelmed by the lush green paradise around me. Brightly colored birds dart through a tangled canopy of leaves and vines. Boa constrictors hang from branches. Lizards and alligators scamper into dense brush lining the shore. In every direction, I hear chaotic choruses of chirps and yelps, whistles and whirrs.

"It's a jungle out there," jokes the guide.

And just ahead are Indians. Friendly ones.

The teen missionaries and I can't wait to meet them. Despite our cultural differences, we hope to win the confidence of the tribe—then win their souls to Christ.

As our canoe pulls up to the shore, a bunch of questions flood my mind: why do I spend so much time clinging to my comfort zones—instead of taking eternal risks for God? When this trip is over, how can I possibly return to a "me-centered life" when Christ has called me to something greater: taking the Gospel to the ends of the earth?

• • •

Lives were changed during that unforgettable jungle adventure—even my own. For the first time, I began to understand what an eternal risk is all about: leaving my comfortable world behind and boldly stepping out as Christ's hands and feet. My experience in Panama instilled in me a heart for the lost and a passion for serving Jesus back home in my own neighborhood.

So, what kinds of risks can *you* take for God?

Tell others about Christ. It's definitely a risk, but a high and noble one. Witnessing means reflecting the love of Jesus through your words and, more importantly, through your actions. (We'll talk more about witnessing in chapter 36.)

Speak the truth. Keeping quiet about creation (or purity or the pro-life cause) is easier, even safer. But speaking up is gutsy—and the right thing to do.

Roll up your sleeves and serve. Jesus gives some great ideas in Matthew 25:31–46. Activities like feeding the hungry, clothing the naked, taking care of the sick, visiting people in prison. Collect old blankets from neighbors and hand them out to homeless families in your town. All around you are people in need of a friend. Your own neighborhood is a great place to start. Help someone who is hurting. Hey, here's an idea: start a neighborhood Bible study.

Healing Steps

Break free from comfort zones. A comfort zone is that invisible, safe circle we put around ourselves so we don't have to be bothered by anything or anyone. It's a selfish, protective cocoon that keeps us from being all God wants us to be.

Believe that the way of Christ is the narrow way (Matthew 7:13–14). Jesus promised His disciples pain and suffering (John 15:18–21), not a life of ease. Our struggle takes place against the evil powers of this dark world (Ephesians 6:12).

Be committed to the adventure of knowing and following Jesus. The fact is, being a Christian is the most exciting, most energizing, most fulfilling adventure anybody could ever hope to embark on. Following Jesus isn't a chore or a hassle. It's a privilege! Does it mean you're going to skip all problems? Of course not. But your heavenly Father wants you to learn how to overcome hardships. In doing so, you'll begin to understand what it really means to step out as a "Christian." Commit right now to trusting Jesus with your whole heart. Ask Him to help you steer clear of the world's lies and to be firmly grounded in His truth.

Healing Words for Growth

Healing Words for My Family (and How I Plan to Use Them):

_____

_____

_____

Healing Words for Growth:

_____

_____

_____

Healing Words to Pray:

_____

_____

_____

32

Ordinary Heroes, Extraordinary Impact

"Then the King will say to those on his right, 'Come, you who are blessed by my Father; take your inheritance, the kingdom prepared for you since the creation of the world. For I was hungry and you gave me something to eat, I was thirsty and you gave me something to drink, I was a stranger and you invited me in, I needed clothes and you clothed me, I was sick and you looked after me, I was in prison and you came to visit me.' "
MATTHEW 25:34–36

A tender word spoken at the right moment, a smile, a simple act of kindness—these are the marks of a true hero. No need for dramatic feats of strength. No need to outrun a speeding bullet or leap over a skyscraper in a single bound.

As a Christian, you're already empowered with supernatural wonder: the Holy Spirit. It's Christ in you and the outpouring of His love through your words, your warmth, and your walk that will rescue humanity from evil. It's the Hero reflected in your face that will open their eyes to eternity.

→ **Are you sharing God's love with those around you?**
What do people see when they look at your life? Humility,
kindness, goodness—a reflection of Christ's face?

Healing Journey

The two main centers of obedience to God are your heart and your mouth. That's why David prayed, "May these words of my mouth and this meditation of my heart be pleasing in your sight, LORD, my Rock and my Redeemer" (Psalm 19:14). He knew that if he could just let his heavenly Father take control of his heart and his mouth, he could live a holy life; a life that would be a testimony to God's glory and grace.

Does your speech encourage and empower—or does it wound and destroy? Do you communicate hope, or do you occasionally spray others with hateful graffiti: insults and put-downs?

Bestselling author Frank Peretti, a man who considers himself to be among the world's "walking wounded," warns Christians to avoid verbal abuse:

> *At some point in a child's life he becomes the inferior one, the different one, the ugly one, the fat one. For whatever reason that shapes the way he interacts. It's like painting a sign around your neck: "Beat up on me because you'll get away with it." You begin to expect to be treated that way, and the other kids pick up on that like an animal smelling prey.*
>
> *That's how it was for me. My teen world was a virtual prison. Here's some advice for Christians of all ages: Have nothing to do with words that wound.[1]*

Matthew 6:21 says, "For where your treasure is, there your heart will be also." In other words, if having money or being popular or gaining power is important to you, that will be the focus of your heart—and that's how people will see you. (You've probably heard comments like, "He's only looking out for number one" or "She's so vain.") Likewise, if knowing and serving Jesus is your priority, it will show in how you treat others.

Use Philippians 4:8 as a guide to what should enter your heart: "Finally, brothers and sisters, whatever is noble, whatever is right, whatever is pure, whatever is lovely, whatever is admirable—if anything is excellent or praiseworthy—think about such things."

Healing Steps

Share random acts of heroism. Need some ideas? Try these: make food for someone; visit people in a nursing home; help a friend clean his room or do homework; buy a meal for a homeless person; invite a friend to youth group; buy a friend a CD (even if it isn't his or her birthday); take neighborhood kids to a baseball game. The idea is to do the unthinkable, something someone might never expect.

Strive to be an encourager. Now more than ever the world needs encouragers—godly people who offer kindness and compassion, heroic people who are willing to reach out to those who have been wounded by discouragers. Ask the Lord to show you how to be merciful, just as He is merciful. Consider this: He reaches out to the unlovable, befriends those the world would rather forget, and touches those who seem untouchable.

Set the example for others. Living a double life is a surefire way to blow your witness—especially to a non-Christian. Remember, others are watching you.

Healing Words for Growth

Healing Words for My Family (and How I Plan to Use Them):

_____

_____

_____

Healing Words for Growth:

_____

_____

_____

Healing Words to Pray:

_____

_____

_____

33

Divine Appointments

*Brothers and sisters, if someone is caught in a sin, you who live
by the Spirit should restore that person gently. But watch yourselves,
or you also may be tempted. Carry each other's burdens,
and in this way you will fulfill the law of Christ.*
GALATIANS 6:1–2

Not only does God expect us to carry each other's burdens, but He actually orchestrates divine appointments, placing needy people in our lives so we can encourage and bless them. So whenever we encounter a hurting neighbor, our prayer should be, "Lord, how can I help? You knew our paths would cross, so what can I do to nudge this person a little closer to You?"

And verse 1 of today's scripture passage reminds us that it's worth putting friendship on the line to help someone in need. Think of it this way: If your friend had a hearing deficit and he was playing in the street, he might not hear danger coming. But if you could see that he was only moments away from becoming a hood ornament, what would your friendship demand of you? You'd have to run into the street—tackle him, knock him over, whatever it took—but you would do your best to get him out of danger.

This is how we should be caring for people in our community.

Perhaps someone is blowing it spiritually and would be blessed by your testimony. Perhaps you have been delivered from what seemed like an insurmountable challenge and can speak truth into a hurting neighbor's circumstances. It may be that God has been purposefully shaping your life in some specific way so that you can now be the kind of person who will carry the burdens of others.[1]

→ Is there someone in your life who needs a helping hand? How
do you react when a friend is making a bad choice? Do you remain
silent, or do you speak up? What if it's a person in authority?

Healing Journey

Twenty-two-year-old Chris was tempted to use drugs by the unlikeliest source—one of his own college professors. During his last semester at a state university in northern California, the Christian young man joined one of his art classes on a field trip to a major graphic design firm in San Jose. (It was about a six-hour drive from their campus.) Many of the students drove their own cars, while Chris and four other students piled into the back of their teacher's pick-up truck. He had a canopy on the back, which meant they were slightly cramped yet cozy!

It was an exciting trip—he and his new friends were laughing and telling stories in the back of the truck. Suddenly their teacher slid open the cab window and handed back some sort of pipe with something burning in it. The odor was sweet and weird, and Chris wasn't sure what it was. His teacher exclaimed, "This will make the trip go by faster!"

One of his fellow students looked at the pipe with a puzzled expression then said, "Pot? Our teacher's doin' drugs?"

Without hesitation, he then handed the pipe to Chris. The young man winced and passed it to the next student. "No thanks," Chris said. "I don't do drugs."

The pipe made its way around the entire group without anyone taking a hit. One of the girls handed it back their teacher.

Slightly confused and perhaps a little bit high, the instructor stuck his head through the window and scowled. "What's the matter with you?" he grumbled. "You're college students! Don't any of you know how to party?"

• • •

Today Chris is thankful that he didn't cave in and end up being a bad witness. And he has discovered through the years that you don't have to get on a soap box or "thump the Bible." Just show a little backbone and take a stand for what you believe. Gently and respectfully point your neighbors to God's truth, and encourage fellow believers to "keep in step with the Spirit" (see Galatians 5:25).

Healing Steps

Stay sane: be responsible to *your neighbor, not* for *them.* In other words, once we've made the effort to steer someone back on course, we must remember that they are the ones who have to make the right choices. All we can do at that point is pray and be available.

Understand that once we put our apprehensions aside and actually do what God wants us to do, we are, in effect, laying down our lives for our friends. When we value our friends over our feelings of embarrassment and stupidity, we are living out the sacrificial love of Jesus. And that's nothing to feel embarrassed or stupid about!

Healing Words for Growth

Healing Words for My Family (and How I Plan to Use Them):

_____

_____

_____

Healing Words for Growth:

_____

_____

_____

Healing Words to Pray:

_____

_____

_____

34

Breaking Free From Our Christian Bubbles

"Go into all the world and preach the gospel to all creation."
MARK 16:15

Living our lives in a "holy huddle" with other Christians makes us feel safe—even comfortable. When our focus is on the huddle, we don't have to deal with scary people on the outside. But here's some amazing news: our comfort has a very low biblical priority.

Jesus isn't as concerned about our comfort. If anything, He calls us to spend time *out* of our holy huddle and to impact the world for Him. Throughout the Gospels we see examples of Christ making His disciples uncomfortable by befriending scary people—outcasts.

True, Jesus doesn't want us to get pulled *down* by the wrong crowd. Instead, He wants us to extend a helping hand and to pull others *up*.

Think about modern-day outcasts: the handicapped kid who is often overlooked or the loner who never leaves her house. Would Jesus visit these people? Would He know their names, care about them, tell them stories? He would—and you should, too. Check out what the Bible says in 2 Corinthians 2:15: "For we are to God the pleasing aroma of Christ among those who are being saved and those who are perishing."

→ **Are you willing to get off your "pew" and get going?**
If so, how do you smell to the world?

Healing Journey

This verse (2 Corinthians 2:15) hit home with a boy in my (Michael's) church youth group several years back. After hearing me read it during Bible study one night, fourteen-year-old Brian was determined to live it out.

A week or so later, the teen showed up at my office with a boy named Ramon. I looked up from my computer. . .and gasped.

This guy's a thug! I thought.

Ramon didn't have a nose ring or a Grateful Dead tattoo engraved on his forehead. But he was rough looking—sort of like the type who made "deals" behind the gym after school. And he smelled like heavy cologne mixed with cigarette smoke.

"What's up?" Ramon said with a half-smile, his eyes surveying my office.

On no, he's casing the place.

Brian grinned at my reaction. "Ramon is joining me at the youth revival tomorrow night."

"No kidding," I said, studying Ramon. "So, Brian says there's a lot of stuff going on in your life. Maybe we could grab a Coke and talk about it sometime. . ."

"Maybe you could come to our Bible study tonight," Brian interrupted.

Ramon nodded.

Brian's smile stretched even bigger.

A short time later, after Ramon left my office, I asked Brian to fill me in on the details.

"What do you suppose Ramon wants from you?" I asked.

"I guess friendship," Brian said. "Maybe a way out from the people he's used to hanging out with. I really want to help him, but I'm not sure how."

Suddenly I was the one grinning from ear to ear. "Brian, you smell pretty good to me."

Brian sniffed his jacket then gave me a puzzled look.

"You are 'the aroma of Christ,' " I explained. "You are His witness in Ramon's life—and that makes you smell amazing!"

Healing Steps

Commit to stepping out of your holy huddle. How? Find an outcast around you—maybe a guy like Ramon—and look for ways that you can affect his or her life. But be careful. While our comfort is a low priority in the Bible, God does expect us to use our brains and avoid stupid risks.

Involve a holy huddle. There's strength in numbers. Trying to impact the life of a "Ramon" can be risky. It helps to get your Christian friends and family involved. Make a team effort to affect your community for Christ. Sometimes it's necessary to get advice from a church leader. Situations could get dangerous, and the person you intended to help could end up pulling you down. Getting counsel and ministering with a group can help you be safer and more effective.

Be a prayer warrior. Praying for the Ramons of this world is the most effective tool to reaching out. After all, God is the One who changes lives.

Healing Words for Growth

Healing Words for My Family (and How I Plan to Use Them):

_____

_____

_____

Healing Words for Growth:

_____

_____

_____

Healing Words to Pray:

_____

_____

_____

35

Love in Action

"My command is this: Love each other as I have loved you. Greater love has no one than this: to lay down one's life for one's friends."
JOHN 15:12–13

In the Bible, the word *love* often refers to action—something we *do* rather than something we *feel*. John 3:16 says, "God so loved the world that he gave. . . ." This verse refers to love as an action, something God did for us. In other places throughout scripture, love is defined as selfless giving to others, as manifesting attitudes of kindness, patience, humility, and commitment in relationships.

> → **How is love expressed in your Christian walk? How does God express His love to you?**

Healing Journey

In John 11:33–44, we witness an amazing act of love: Jesus raising Lazarus from the dead. But focus on verses 33–35 and you catch a clear picture of the Lord's personality: "When Jesus saw her weeping, and the Jews who had come along with her also weeping, he was deeply moved in spirit and troubled. 'Where have you laid him?' he asked. 'Come and see, Lord,' they replied. Jesus wept."

In this passage, Jesus is deeply moved. And every time He is filled with sadness, it's because the people around Him are overcome with mourning. Could it be any clearer how deeply Jesus loves us, how strongly He feels for us? If we're hurting, God is hurting. He is constantly at our side, loving us and encouraging us. He is always there, feeling what we're feeling. He's excited over our victories, and He aches over our defeats.[1]

Although our ability to love is limited, God's capacity to love is endless. Jesus Christ took His infinite love all the way to the cross to lay down His life for His friends—to make a final sacrifice that washes away our sins for all eternity. That's ultimate love in action.

Healing Steps

Learn to love unconditionally. Our love for others is evidence of our love for God. And when we love others unconditionally—forgiving them and reaching out to them—we can approach Jesus confidently in prayer. We can be assured that our prayers will be heard (1 John 5:14).

Communicate ultimate love. Tell others that God is love and He sent His Son to save us from our sin. Christ was the Lamb of God slain for us, who rose from the dead and now lives on the throne. Through His grace we know He will touch and heal our pain and give us strength to meet each day. With the shield of faith and the sword of the Word we will win the fight. Our foe will not beat us when we stand firm and true.

Demonstrate ultimate love. Share the love you experience through Christ with your friends—just as Jesus laid down His life for His friends. Let your speech and actions be a clear message of God's salvation and grace and love.

Healing Words for Growth

Healing Words for My Family (and How I Plan to Use Them):

_____

_____

_____

Healing Words for Growth:

_____

_____

_____

Healing Words to Pray:

_____

_____

_____

36

Three Stories: A Way to Witness

You yourselves are our letter, written on our hearts, known and read by everyone. You show that you are a letter from Christ, the result of our ministry, written not with ink but with the Spirit of the living God, not on tablets of stone but on tablets of human hearts.
2 CORINTHIANS 3:2–3

While our Savior's first call is to "Come, follow me" (Matthew 4:19), His second is to "Go"—"Go into all the world and preach the gospel to all creation" (Mark 16:15).

But the truth is, most Christians are way too uptight about witnessing. We fear we'll mess up what God accomplished through the cross. We obsess over appearances. We treat those outside the faith like projects instead of people. We speak an alien language—known by insiders as "Christianese." The best thing we can do is relax and live what we believe, naturally, honestly, comfortably.

→ **Exactly how are we to accomplish this? How can we get past the fear, take off the masks—and let people see the real, eternity-bound person inside? How can others encounter the Savior through our lives?**

Healing Journey

I (Michael) was on Interstate 40 just west of Knoxville, Tennessee. It was late, and the snow was coming down so hard I could barely see the taillights of my friend's Jeep. I was supposed to be following him to Gatlinburg, a popular mountain resort, but I was having trouble keeping up.

In less than twenty-four hours, I was scheduled to stand on a stage in front of six thousand winter-retreating teenagers. I was there to cohost a glitzy New Year's Eve celebration with big names like Josh McDowell and Toby Mac. (That is, if I made it.)

Suddenly my rental car hit a patch of ice and veered right, dangerously close to a drop-off. I twisted the wheel into the slide, then turned left—correcting the spinout and avoiding disaster. But as my heart rate returned to normal, I discovered that I had become separated from my friend.

He's probably pulling into Gatlinburg right now, I told myself. *I've had enough of this icy road craziness. Time to call it a night.*

I spotted a Denny's sign and decided to make a detour. A quick meal, directions to a motel, a good night's sleep—my plan was set. Little did I realize God had another purpose for my unexpected pit stop.

"You're smart for pulling in," a young waiter assured me as he slid a cup of coffee across my table. "You'd never make it tonight—the roads are bad."

I nodded and stirred cream into my hot drink. The waiter paused then sat down at my booth.

"May I ask you a question?" he said with a serious tone.

"Uh—sure," I responded.

"I overheard you talking to another waiter," he said. "You mentioned that you're speaking at the youth event in Gatlinburg. It's a big deal every New Year's. It's always advertised on the radio."

I nodded my head again and took a sip of coffee.

"It's a Christian event," he continued, "so I assume you're a Christian."

"Yes, I am."

"Why?" he asked, looking me in the eyes. "I mean, I'm not religious—and I don't plan to be. But I've got to know something. How has being a Christian changed your life?"

Slightly shocked, slightly overjoyed, I nearly choked on my coffee. I swallowed hard then cleared my throat.

"Well, uh—do you have all night?" I asked. The young man smiled and folded his arms. I took another sip of coffee and began.

"First of all, I'm not religious either. I have a relationship—a relationship with Jesus Christ. He's changed my life in lots of ways: He's given me hope, purpose. . .eternity with Him. He's forgiven me for all the stupid things I've ever done or thought. He's shown me what love—*real* love—is all about."

As I talked, and as this young waiter listened, I forgot about the snow piling up outside and the next day's big youth event. The only thing that seemed to matter was that moment—and that person.

I talked from the heart, and he listened. It was as simple as that. I didn't use big words or debate lofty doctrines or worry about impressing this guy. I merely told my story and gave him a glimpse of my life.

About thirty cups of coffee later, the waiter pointed to his watch. "It's getting late, and the weather looks pretty bad," he said. "I'll let you go so you can find a motel for the night. Thanks for talking with me. I've got a lot to think about."

I smiled and shook his hand. "You asked some good questions. Don't stop doing that."

As I headed out the door and trudged through the snow, hoping I said all the right things, I experienced a kind of icy road awakening. *Lord, I get it. It's not just about "winning" someone's salvation. It's about genuinely "loving my neighbors." It's about keeping my heart in tune with You so You can work through me. And it's really about living in a way that points others to eternity.*

• • •

God doesn't want us to hide our faith from others. Our time on earth is short, but eternity lasts. . .well, *forever*! Therefore, He is counting on us to share the Good News. That could mean going next door and telling your neighbor about Jesus or making Him known to your friends at work or even within your own family. Let God's love shine through your life so others will come to Him.

Here are three essential elements of every person's testimony:

1. *My Story.* Tell very simply how you met Jesus, why you have committed your life to Him, and how He is changing your life—just as I shared during my "icy road awakening."

2. *Your Story.* Relate your own testimony to the circumstances of the person you are witnessing to. Talk about something you have in common, struggles and challenges you're both facing, and how Jesus can bring help, healing, and transformation.

3. *God's Story.* Now tie the three stories together—*my story* (your own), *your story* (your neighbor's), and *God's story* (the plan of salvation). Use five short texts from the book of Romans as a guide.

Romans 3:23: "All have sinned and fall short of the glory of God."

Romans 6:23: "For the wages of sin is death, but the gift of God is eternal life in Christ Jesus our Lord."

Romans 10:9: "If you declare with your mouth, 'Jesus is Lord,' and believe in your heart that God raised him from the dead, you will be saved."

Romans 5:1: "Therefore, since we have been justified through faith, we have peace with God through our Lord Jesus Christ."

Romans 12:2: "Do not conform to the pattern of this world, but be transformed by the renewing of your mind."

Healing Steps

Take a genuine interest in others—instead of treating people like projects. "Jesus replied: ' "Love the Lord your God with all your heart and with all your soul and with all your mind." This is the first and greatest commandment. And the second is like it: 'Love your neighbor as yourself' " (Matthew 22:37–39).

Don't be afraid to speak up—instead of keeping quiet. "Always be prepared to give an answer to everyone who asks you to give the reason for the hope that you have" (1 Peter 3:15).

Allow the Holy Spirit to touch your neighbors through you—instead of blending into the crowd. Too many Christians want to be members of God's secret service, so their speech and actions are no different from those of nonbelievers. And when God becomes the topic of conversation, they clam up. Instead, strive to be different: "Do your best to present yourself to God as one approved, a workman who does not need to be ashamed and who correctly handles the word of truth" (2 Timothy 2:15).

And to be effective witnesses, Christians need to. . .

Know what we believe and why by plugging into the Holy Bible daily. (We can't share with others what we don't know.)

Believe what we know by trusting Jesus Christ daily. (We can't convince others of something we doubt.)

Live what we know and believe by consistently "practicing what we preach." (We can't say one thing then live another way.)

And as you witness, take the time to "check your pulse" from time to time. Ask yourself these questions:

- *What's my motive when I witness?*
- *Is my faith growing, or am I currently stagnate?*
- *Can others see Jesus through my lifestyle?*

Healing Words for Growth

Healing Words for My Family (and How I Plan to Use Them):

_____

_____

_____

Healing Words for Growth:

_____

_____

_____

Healing Words to Pray:

_____

_____

_____

37

Leading the Way

*"Whoever wants to become great among you must be your servant,
and whoever wants to be first must be your slave—just as
the Son of Man did not come to be served, but to serve."*
MATTHEW 20:26–28

Being a Christ-follower also means being a servant leader in your community. And men and women who lead the way possess five distinct character qualities.

- *They strive to love God with all their hearts, minds, and souls.*
- *They lay down their lives for others.*
- *They humble themselves, taking on the very nature of a servant.*
- *They nurture love, joy, peace, patience, kindness, goodness, faithfulness, gentleness, self-control.*
- *They walk with honor, integrity, and holiness.*
- *According to A. W. Tozer, if the Church is to prosper spiritually it must have spiritual leadership, not leadership by majority vote.*

It is highly significant that when the apostle Paul found it necessary to ask for obedience among the young churches he never appealed to them on the grounds that he had been duly elected to office," Tozer writes. "He asserted his authority as an apostle appointed by the Head of the church. He held his position by right of sheer spiritual ascendancy, the only earthly right that should be honored among the children of the new creation.[1]

→ Regardless of your profession, regardless of your gifts
and talent, what do you suppose are the characteristics you
possess that are most valued by God? What do you think He
is trying to nurture in you? Most important of all, what will it
take for you to be a man or a woman who is set apart by God,
a Christ-follower who leads the way in your community?

Healing Journey

Imagine yourself blasting into outer space. As the orbiter rockets four to five times the speed of sound, your body is pressed back into your seat. (You actually now weigh twice your normal weight—ugh!)

Now imagine that thundering plume of fire and smoke taking you to an orbiting space station or maybe even to Mars. Best of all, you're a bright young woman *and* an astronaut, excelling in a field once dominated by men. Even better: you're a woman of faith, a servant God is using to fulfill His eternal plans.

If being this kind of servant leader is your desire, it can happen—just ask shuttle astronaut Shannon Lucid. She holds down the fort in Houston, where she's a wife and mother of two daughters and one son. She was also part of NASA's space shuttle team and served as a mission specialist. For more than two decades, she was an elite member of those who had "the right stuff."

"It was truly a dream come true for me," she says. "I was hired by NASA in 1978 and went on my first mission aboard *Discovery*. Ever since I can remember, I wanted to be an astronaut.

"As a young woman, I was a real oddball," Shannon continues. "When I went to high school and college, everyone expected girls to do one thing: grow up and be housewives. This is a noble pursuit, and I ended up becoming one too—at least part-time. But I knew God had other plans for me, as well. I knew it involved space exploration."

With the direction of her Lord and the support of her husband and family, Shannon set off into the great unknown—literally! (During her career she logged more than a thousand hours in space.)

"But if God isn't behind it," she points out, "I wouldn't be either." This, she says, should be a Christian's most important desire: becoming the leader God desires; the one who sets the standard.[2]

Healing Steps

Be patient as God molds you. As popular author Henry T. Blackaby points out, "He will take whatever time is necessary to grow your character to match

His assignment for you. . . . Character-building can be long and painful. It took twenty-five years before God entrusted Abraham with his first son and set in motion the establishment of the nation of Israel. Yet God was true to His Word."[3]

Allow the Holy Spirit and the truth of the Bible to saturate your heart, mind, and soul. This is an essential key to building leadership. Here's how pastor and author David Jeremiah explains it: "God will not prostitute His power to give us desires that will in the end be destructive to our walk with Him. But if we are consumed with a passion to find God's will through His Word and His Holy Spirit, we can always be in the place where God can shower down His power upon us."[4]

Ask God to mold you. Pray this: "Lord, shape my character as You prepare me to fulfill Your purpose." Ask Jesus to grow you into a young woman who is far stronger, far more obedient than you presently are. Ask Him to show you how to be faithful with the small assignments—always preparing you to handle even bigger tasks.

Healing Words for Growth

Healing Words for My Family (and How I Plan to Use Them):

_____

_____

_____

Healing Words for Growth:

_____

_____

_____

Healing Words to Pray:

_____

_____

_____

38

Powerful Words That Open Doors

Jesus had the most open and all-encompassing mind that this world has ever seen. His own inner conviction was so strong, so firm, so unswerving that He could afford to mingle with any group secure in the knowledge that He would not be contaminated. It is fear that makes us unwilling to listen to another's point of view, fear that our own ideas may be attacked. Jesus had no such fear, no such pettiness of viewpoint, no need to fence Himself off for His own protection. He knew the difference between graciousness and compromise, and we would do well to learn from Him. He set for us the most magnificent and glowing example of truth combined with mercy of all time, and in departing said: "Go ye and do likewise" (Luke 10:37).

BILLY GRAHAM[1]

God Heals the *Brokenhearted*

Psalm 147:3: "He heals the brokenhearted and binds up their wounds."
How to Open Doors: Think about the people in your community—your barber or hair stylist down the street, the clerk at the corner pharmacy, your neighbor next door. Chances are, each one is navigating his or her own long list of challenges and could use an encouraging word from you. Consider sharing these five truths about God:

1. He is close to the brokenhearted.
2. He struggles with us as we struggle.
3. He uses pain in our lives to strengthen us.
4. He gives us the strength to endure any problem.
5. He is our healer.

God Heals the *Lost*

Isaiah 53:5: "He was pierced for our transgressions, he was crushed for our iniquities; the punishment that brought us peace was on him, and by his wounds we are healed."

How to Open Doors: Think about all that Jesus Christ has freely done for believers. He has forgiven our sin and freed us from the bondage of death, and He promises eternal life with Him. This is the Gospel, the ultimate Good News—and it's exactly what our neighbors need to hear. Pray for your community and be ready to share how your neighbors can know Jesus personally:

- Agree that your *sin* keeps you from having a personal relationship with God (Romans 3:23).
- Believe that *Jesus Christ* died on a cross and rose again so that your sins could be forgiven (1 Peter 3:18).
- Accept God's gift of *grace*. You must also trust Jesus to be your Savior and to forgive you of your sins (John 1:12).
- Understand that you have the promise of eternal life with Him and a *crown of righteousness* (1 John 5:13).
- Trust Jesus and begin a *new life* in Him! You can grow in His love, peace, strength, and knowledge. Begin your great adventure now by letting Him guide every step you take (2 Peter 3:18).
- Pray: "Lord Jesus, I agree that I am a sinner who is separated from God. And I know that You have forgiven my sins and offer me the gift of eternal life. I accept this awesome gift. Come into my life right now, fill me with your Holy Spirit, and cleanse me. Make me the person you want me to be. I commit my life to You right now. From this day forward, I give You control. I now live for You. Amen."

God Heals Those Who *Revere* His Name

Malachi 4:2: "For you who revere my name, the sun of righteousness will rise with healing in its rays. And you will go out and frolic like well-fed calves."

How to Open Doors: In Colossians 2:2–3, the apostle Paul writes: "My goal is that they may be encouraged in heart and united in love, so that they may have the full riches of complete understanding, in order that they may know the mystery of God, namely, Christ, in whom are hidden all the treasures of wisdom and knowledge." Share with your neighbors ten assurances about Christ.

- He can be trusted.
- He is all-powerful.
- He is infinite.
- He is in control.
- He is the Source of truth.
- He accepts you.
- He loves you.
- He forgives you.
- He has an amazing plan for your life.
- He invites you to spend eternity with Him.

God Heals the *Sick*

Matthew 9:35: "Jesus went through all the towns and villages, teaching in their synagogues, proclaiming the good news of the kingdom and healing every disease and sickness."

How to Open Doors: According to Eugene H. Peterson in *Earth and Altar*, "Miracles are not interruptions of laws, which must then ether be denied by worried intellectuals or defended by anxious apologists; they are expressions of freedom enjoyed by the children of a wise and exuberant Father. We do not solve these things with rigorous exegesis of the biblical test or with controlled experiments in a laboratory; we pray them and in praying enter into dimensions of personal freedom in the universe."2 As you encounter the sick in your community, share this:

- God created the universe.
- God parted the waters of the Red Sea.
- God raised His Son from the dead.
- God heals the sick.
- God gives believers a new spiritual life.
- God is the Author of miracles.

God Heals Those Who *Suffer*

Mark 5:34: "[Jesus] said to her, 'Daughter, your faith has healed you. Go in peace and be freed from your suffering.' "

How to Open Doors: When you encounter someone in your community who is suffering, explain this: "As we trust God completely, He works things out perfectly. It's easy to allow ourselves to be overly concerned about the unknown as we suffer. But the challenges we face really aren't our problems. They are God's. He will take care of us. The Lord has armed every Christian with spiritual weapons packed with divine power":

- The sword of the Spirit—the Holy Bible.
- Prayer. Colossians 3:16 (NASB) tells Christ-followers to "let the word of Christ richly dwell within you."
- Supernatural peace. Philippians 4:7 promises that "the peace of God. . .will guard your hearts and your minds in Christ Jesus."

Christ-Followers, Plant These Words and Grow

Nourish spiritual growth with God's Word. Ezekiel, a Jewish priest who was exiled in Babylon, wrote these inspired words from God: "I will give you a new heart and put a new spirit within you; I will take the heart of stone out of your flesh and give you a heart of flesh. I will put My Spirit within you and cause you to walk in My statutes, and you will keep My judgments and do *them*" (Ezekiel 36:26–27 NKJV).

A righteous walk with Christ begins with a transformed heart. When Jesus takes hold of our hearts and begins making radical changes within us, He gives us a desire to follow His examples in word and deed—to see others the way He sees them, to forgive, to love, to lay down our lives for the cause of Christ. . .to *go* into all the world and share the Good News. Jesus gives us the confidence, the strength, and the discernment we need to fulfill His will.

As Billy Graham has pointed out, Jesus Christ has set for us the most magnificent and glowing example of truth combined with mercy of all time. And one of the greatest things we can do for our communities, he explains, is to point men, women, and children to the timeless instruction of the Bible.

"Millions of people today are searching for a reliable voice of authority," says Graham. "The Word of God is the only real authority we have. His Word sheds light on human nature, world problems and human suffering. But beyond that, it clearly reveals the way to God. . . .When we read God's Word, we fill our hearts with His words, and God is speaking to us."[3]

In the days ahead, do the following:

Plot a course for growth. List your goals:
In one month I want to. . .
In six months I want to. . .
In one year I want to. . .

List ten steps that you will take to grow (and reach your goals above):

1. _____
2. _____
3. _____
4. _____
5. _____
6. _____
7. _____
8. _____
9. _____
10. _____

39

Powerful Words That Erase the Hate

Darkness cannot drive out darkness; only light can do that.
Hate cannot drive out hate; only love can do that. . . . We must
develop and maintain the capacity to forgive. He who is devoid
of the power to forgive is devoid of the power to love. There is
some good in the worst of us and some evil in the best of us.
When we discover this, we are less prone to hate our enemies.
MARTIN LUTHER KING JR.[1]

God Wants Every Race to *Coexist*

1 John 3:15: "Anyone who hates a brother or sister is a murderer, and you know that no murderer has eternal life residing in him."

How to Erase the Hate: As you strive to promote peace and unity in your community, communicate this: God populated the world with thousands of ethnic groups. According to the U.S. Center for World Mission in Pasadena, California, there are five major races (Australoid, Capoid, Caucasian, Oriental, Negroid), seven colors (black, white, yellow, red, tan, brown, gray), 432 major peoples, 9,000 distinct ethnic groups and more than 6,170 languages.[2] Incredible, isn't it? What's even more awesome is that God knows every man, woman, and child personally.

God Made Us *Equal*—and Judges Us Equally

Romans 2:6–11: "God 'will repay each person according to what they have done.' To those who by persistence in doing good seek glory, honor and immortality, he will give eternal life. But for those who are self-seeking and who reject the truth and follow evil, there will be wrath and anger. There will be trouble and distress for every human being who does evil: first for the Jew, then for the Gentile; but glory, honor and peace for everyone who does good: first for the Jew, then for the Gentile. For God does not show favoritism."

How to Erase the Hate: Here's a question to ponder: since racism spreads hatred and destruction, would God ever tolerate it? The answer, of course, is no! (The scripture verses above makes this clear.) The saying "God didn't make junk" is absolutely true. We are all equal and very special in His eyes. He wants to give eternal life to every man, woman, and child.

"God *Loves* Us Unconditionally"

Ephesians 5:1–2: "Follow God's example, therefore, as dearly loved children and walk in the way of love."

How to Erase the Hate: God wants us to love one another unconditionally and to live in peace. And when it comes to racism, He wants us to be "barrier busters." The word barrier is another name for wall, and there are basically only two ways we can break down walls. (Three if your name is Joshua and you know seven priests who play ram's horns, but this can get complicated [see Joshua 6:4–5].) A smart way to break down a wall is to remove one brick at a time. It takes time and patience, it takes a lot of work, and it requires hand-to-hand involvement. But it's worth it. And as Christians who worship a God of justice and love, we should be angry about racism—and, therefore, strive to break down walls between the races. Remember this: walls go up one brick at a time, and they can come down one brick at a time, too.

"God Brings Healing to the *Repentant*"

Hosea 14:4: "I will heal their waywardness and love them freely, for my anger has turned away from them."

How to Erase the Hate: As you reach out to members of your community—leading them to a relationship with Jesus Christ— encourage them to take three faith-building steps that will, in turn, help them to tear down walls of hate.

1. *Accept Christ's forgiveness.* Say this: "Whenever we blow it in some way, we can go to the Lord in prayer. Confess our sin, ask for forgiveness, and press ahead with the power of the Lord."

2. *Learn from our mistakes.* Explain that God wants us to practice avoiding the traps that cause us to stumble, which includes judging others by the color of their skin.

3. *Forgive others.* Explain that it's our responsibility to forgive as Christ has forgiven us. Say this: "Has somebody wronged you? Are you harboring bitterness? Don't delay. Go to that person and strive to work through the problem. Above all, forgive as God forgives."

Christ-Followers, Plant These Words and Grow

Nourish spiritual growth with God's Word. First John 4:19–21 says, "We love because he first loved us. Whoever claims to love God yet hates a brother or sister is a liar. For whoever does not love their brother and sister, whom they have seen, cannot love God, whom they have not seen. And he has given us this command: Anyone who loves God must also love their brother and sister."

As a Christ-follower, you can express love by developing relationships with people who are different from you. Get to know them as friends, do things together, serve one another. Little by little, through your example, people will begin to notice that the perceived walls that once divided us aren't as high as they once thought they were. They will actually begin to realize that they don't need to be trapped on either side of them.

As Martin Luther King Jr. pointed out, there is some good in the worst of us and some evil in the best of us. Yet, in his words, "the ultimate measure of a man is not where he stands in moments of comfort and convenience, but where he stands at times of challenge and controversy." Where do you stand with the issue of racial or religious hate? Keep in mind that everybody can be great, because everybody can tear down the walls and serve. "You don't have to have a college degree to serve," Dr. King said. "You don't have to make your subject and verb agree to serve. You only need a heart full of grace. A soul generated by love."[3]

In the days ahead, do the following:

Plot a course for growth. List your goals:
In one month I want to. . .
In six months I want to. . .
In one year I want to. . .

List ten steps that you will take to grow (and reach your goals above):
1. _____
2. _____
3. _____
4. _____
5. _____
6. _____
7. _____
8. _____
9. _____
10. _____

40

Ready to Rethink Community and Start Serving Our Neighbors?

We know that God loves us and that we should love God. But there is no way I would characterize most Christians or most churches by their love for God. People in love act much differently than people with a sense of obligation. People do crazy things for love. Love has a way of making even the most difficult tasks feel simple and joyful. It has a way of pushing us to act with complete abandon and devotion.

FRANCIS CHAN[1]

Chart a Healing Path toward Change

1. *Receive God's Word:* Read or listen to John 15:1–17.

2. *Reflect on John 15:9–11:* Pull these verses apart sentence by sentence, looking for God's personal message to you. Invite the Holy Spirit to speak to you.

> *"As the Father has loved me, so have I loved you. Now remain in my love. If you obey my commands, you will remain in my love, just as I have obeyed my Father's commands and remain in his love. I have told you this so that my joy may be in you and that your joy may be complete."*

3. *Engage in a conversation with God.* After a moment of silence before the Lord, write out a dialogue between you and Him. Begin with general thoughts and impressions.

Heavenly Father, here's how I feel about these verses:

_____

_____

_____

Here's what's hard for me, God—what I don't understand:

_____

_____

_____

Now relate these verses to your specific circumstances.

Here's what John 15:1–17 is telling me about Christ's love:

_____

_____

_____

With your help, Lord, here's the kind of radical love I want to express to You and to my neighbors:

_____

_____

_____

4. *Memorize John 15:12–13.* Repeat it to yourself as often as needed. Write it on an index card and post it a public place.

"My command is this: Love each other as I have loved you. Greater love has no one than this: to lay down one's life for one's friends."

5. *Respond to God's nudges.* Try this "Community Love" exercise:

- First, read what pastor and author David A. Busic has to say about affecting our community for Jesus Christ: "You are not where you are by accident. Not in your neighborhood, not at your work, not at your school. God is continually orchestrating divine appointments, intersecting your path with people who need to experience God's love. All He is asking from you is obedience. It may not always make sense, but we cannot afford to hesitate. There is too much at stake.[2]

Now think of people God wants you to love. . .

* that cantankerous neighbor across the street
* a single-parent dad at church
* the nameless people who beg for money on street corners.
* the broken, the addicted, the unlovely—the scary folks who wouldn't dare set foot in church.
* Next, ask God these questions: *What must I do? How can I be Your hands and feet in my community—Your face to those I encounter? How can I love them?*

Notes

Starting Point: How to Live What James Taught

1. Dirk R. Buursma, *Daylight Devotional Bible* (Grand Rapids: Zondervan, 1988), 1323.

1. Acting as If We've Been Baptized in Lemon Juice (and Other Ways We Repel People)

1. These statistics are compiled from a seven-year survey-based spiritual research study conducted by Back to the Bible and goTandem. For more information, visit www.backtothebible.org.

4. Hospital Mentality vs. Country Club Mentality

1. David Wilkerson, *Victory over Sin and Self* (Grand Rapids: Revell, 1994), 23.

5. Creating a Safe Harbor for Everyone

1. Max Lucado, *The Great House of God* (Nashville: Word, 1997), x.

7. Navigating the Fear Factor

1. Charles H. Spurgeon, *Morning and Evening* (Nashville: Thomas Nelson, 1994), December 28, evening.

8. Loving Words for Unlovely People

1. William Arthur Ward, "William Arthur Ward Quotes," ThinkExist. com, http://thinkexist.com/quotes/William_Arthur_Ward/.

9. Loving Words for Laymen and Leaders

1. Eugene O'Neill, *The Great God Brown* (Grand Rapids: Chosen, 2010), 58.

10. Ready to Rethink Church and Start Living What Christ Intended?

1. Mother Teresa, "Mother Teresa Quotes," from *A Gift for God*,

NotableQuotes, http://www.notable-quotes.com/t/teresa_mother.html.

11. It's Time to Be a Cubicle Missionary

1. Dan Boone, *The Way We Work: How Faith Makes a Difference on the Job* (Kansas City: Beacon Hill, 2014), 11–12.

2. Bob Briner, *Roaring Lambs: A Gentle Plan to Radically Change Your World* (Grand Rapids: Zondervan, 1993), 18–19.

3. Dirk Buursma, *Daylight Devotional Bible* (Grand Rapids: Zondervan, 1988), 699.

4. Quote taken from Michael and Tiffany Ross, *Does Mastercard Accept Visa?* (Kansas City: Beacon Hill, 2003), 23.

5. Thomas à Kempis, *The Imitation of Christ* (San Francisco: HarperCollins, 2000), 6.

12. Unlock a Dream

1. John Eldredge, *Dare to Desire* (Nashville: Thomas Nelson, 2002), 3.

13. Secrets of a Ragamuffin Worker: What We Can Learn from Manning and Mullins

1. Brennan Manning, *The Ragamuffin Gospel: Embracing the Unconditional Love of God* (Colorado Springs: Multnomah, 1990), 50.

2. Ibid., 69.

3. Les Sussman, *Praise Him! Christian Music Stars Share Their Favorite Verses from Scripture* (New York: St. Martin's, 1998), 155–64.

4. Christopher Coppernoll, *Soul2Soul* (Nashville: W, 1998), 47, 49.

14. Holding Your Tongue and Turning Your Cheek

1. C. S. Lewis, *Mere Christianity* (New York: HarperCollins, 2001), 121–22.

2. *Serendipity Bible* (Grand Rapids: Zondervan, 1988), 1431.

15. "But I Feel Like a Christian Doormat" (When and How to Speak Up)

1. Spurgeon, *Morning and Evening*, December 28, evening.

2. Paul Coughlin, *No More Christian Nice Guy: When Being Nice—Instead of Good—Hurts Men, Women, and Children* (Minneapolis: Bethany House, 2005), 149–51.

3. Ibid., 153.

4. Manfred Koehler, "Why Christians Suffer," *Breakaway*, March 2001, 30.

16. Shared Meaning: A Transformational Communication Style

1. This portion of the chapter is adapted from Michael Ross and Tess Cox, *Dating, Relating, Waiting: God's Word on Purity* (Uhrichsville, OH: Barbour, 2015), 73–75.

17. Ten Basics of Workplace Evangelism

1. C. S. Lewis, *God in the Dock: Essays on Theology and Ethics* (Grand Rapids: Eerdmans, 1970), 128.

18. Kind Words for Mean Bosses

1. Boone, *The Way We Work: How Faith Makes a Difference on the Job*, 83.
2. Ibid., 88–89.

19. Kind Words for Cantankerous Colleagues

1. Coughlin, *No More Christian Nice Guy: When Being Nice—Instead of Good—Hurts Men, Women, and Children*, 152.

2. Ibid., 152–53.

20. Ready to Rethink the Workplace and Start Walking Our Witness?

1. Bob Briner, *Roaring Lambs: A Gentle Plan to Radically Change Your World* (Grand Rapids: Zondervan, 1993), 47.

2. Information in this chart was inspired by Robert S. McGee, *The Search for Significance* (Nashville: Word, 1998), 28–29. We highly recommend reading this excellent resource.

21. Building a Stress-less Home

1. This story is adapted from Arnie Cole and Michael Ross, *Unstuck: Your Life, God's Design, Real Change* (Minneapolis: Bethany House, 2012), 137–38.

2. Dr. Pam Ovwigho, executive research director at Back to the Bible, contributed the information in this section.

22. Resolving Conflict: The Ephesians 4:26 Principle

1. Adapted from Michael Ross and Susie Shellenberger, *What Your Son Isn't Telling You: Unlocking the Secret World of Teen Boys* (Minneapolis: Bethany House, 2010), 47–48.

24. What to Say When Families Fracture

1. Edmund Bourne, PhD, *Coping with Anxiety* (Oakland, CA: New Harbinger, 2003), 44.

2. Ibid.

25. Father Hunger: Healing Messages Kids Need

1. Paul W. Swets, *The Art of Talking with Your Teenager* (Holbrook, MA: Adams, 1995), 16.

27. Essential Words for Wives

1. Sara Groves. Quote obtained from interview with Michael Ross, June 2003.

28. Essential Words for Husbands

1. Dr. James Dobson, "A Man and His Ultimate Priority," James Dobson's Family Talk, 2014, http://drjamesdobson.org/articles/families-on-the-front-lines/a-man-and-his-ultimate-priority.

2. Kristi Winkler, "10 Bible Verses for Father's Day," Sharefaith.com, June 2, 2014, http://www.sharefaith.com/blog/2014/06/10-bible-verses-fathers-day-scripture-based-descriptions-father/.

29. Essential Words for Children

1. Lady Bird Johnson, "Famous Quotes about Children," Compassion International, 2015, http://www.compassion.com/child-advocacy/find-your-voice/famous-quotes/.

30. Ready to Rethink Our Connections with Family and Start Giving More to the Ones We Love?

1. Amy Mandelker and Elizabeth Powers, *Pilgrim Souls* (New York: Simon & Schuster, 1999), 120.

31. Go Ahead—Take an "Eternal Risk"

1. Max Lucado, *Walking with the Savior* (Wheaton, IL: Tyndale House, 1993), 272.

32. Ordinary Heroes, Extraordinary Impact

1. Tom Neven, "Teenage Torture," *Breakaway*, October 2002, 6.

33. Divine Appointments

1. Henry T. Blackaby and Richard Blackaby, *Experiencing God Day-By-Day* (Nashville: Broadman & Holman, 1998), 181.

35. Love in Action

1. Bill Myers, and Michael Ross, *Faith Encounter* (Eugene, OR: Harvest House, 1999), 147.

37. Leading the Way

1. A. W. Tozer, *Tozer on Christian Leadership* (Camp Hill, PA: Christian Publications, 2001), March 4 devotional entry.

2. This story was compiled from an interview with Shannon Lucid conducted by Michael Ross, June 1990.

3. Blackaby and Blackaby, *Experiencing God Day-By-Day*, 16.

4. David Jeremiah, *Sanctuary* (Nashville: Integrity, 2002), 53.

38. Powerful Words That Open Doors

1. Billy Graham, *Unto the Hills* (Nashville: Word, 1986), 123–24.

2. Eugene H. Peterson, *Earth and Altar* (Downers Grove, IL: InterVarsity, 1985), 43.

3. Billy Graham, quoted in Henrietta C. Mears, *What the Bible Is All About* (Ventura, CA: Regal, 1998), 11–12.

39. Powerful Words That Erase the Hate

1. Martin Luther King Jr., "Quotes," BrainyQuote, http://www.brainyquote.com/quotes/authors/m/martin_luther_king_jr.html.

2. U.S. Center for World Mission, "Who Are the Unreached?" 2012–2013, https://www.uscwm.org/.

3. Martin Luther King Jr., "Quotes," Goodreads, http://www.goodreads.com/author/quotes/23924.Martin_Luther_King_Jr_.

40. Ready to Rethink Community and Start Serving Our Neighbors?

1. Francis Chan, *Living Crazy Love: An Interactive Workbook for Individual or Small-Group Study* (Colorado Springs: David C Cook, 2011), 35.

2. David A. Busic, *Perfectly Imperfect: Character Sketches from the New Testament* (Kansas City: Beacon Hill, 2014), 118.

Also available from goTandem:

Available wherever Christian books are sold.